China's Interests and Goals In the Arctic: Implications for the United States

By

Elizabeth Wishnick

March 2017

China's Interests and Goals in the Arctic: Implications for the United States
ISBN: 978-1548004279
Printed in the U.S.A.

The United States Army War College

The United States Army War College educates and develops leaders for service at the strategic level while advancing knowledge in the global application of Landpower.

The purpose of the United States Army War College is to produce graduates who are skilled critical thinkers and complex problem solvers. Concurrently, it is our duty to the U.S. Army to also act as a "think factory" for commanders and civilian leaders at the strategic level worldwide and routinely engage in discourse and debate concerning the role of ground forces in achieving national security objectives.

The Strategic Studies Institute publishes national security and strategic research and analysis to influence policy debate and bridge the gap between military and academia.

The Center for Strategic Leadership contributes to the education of world class senior leaders, develops expert knowledge, and provides solutions to strategic Army issues affecting the national security community.

The Peacekeeping and Stability Operations Institute provides subject matter expertise, technical review, and writing expertise to agencies that develop stability operations concepts and doctrines.

The School of Strategic Landpower develops strategic leaders by providing a strong foundation of wisdom grounded in mastery of the profession of arms, and by serving as a crucible for educating future leaders in the analysis, evaluation, and refinement of professional expertise in war, strategy, operations, national security, resource management, and responsible command.

The U.S. Army Heritage and Education Center acquires, conserves, and exhibits historical materials for use to support the U.S. Army, educate an international audience, and honor Soldiers—past and present.

STRATEGIC STUDIES INSTITUTE

The Strategic Studies Institute (SSI) is part of the U.S. Army War College and is the strategic-level study agent for issues related to national security and military strategy with emphasis on geostrategic analysis.

The mission of SSI is to use independent analysis to conduct strategic studies that develop policy recommendations on:

- Strategy, planning, and policy for joint and combined employment of military forces;

- Regional strategic appraisals;

- The nature of land warfare;

- Matters affecting the Army's future;

- The concepts, philosophy, and theory of strategy; and,

- Other issues of importance to the leadership of the Army.

Studies produced by civilian and military analysts concern topics having strategic implications for the Army, the Department of Defense, and the larger national security community.

In addition to its studies, SSI publishes special reports on topics of special or immediate interest. These include edited proceedings of conferences and topically oriented roundtables, expanded trip reports, and quick-reaction responses to senior Army leaders.

The Institute provides a valuable analytical capability within the Army to address strategic and other issues in support of Army participation in national security policy formulation.

Strategic Studies Institute
and
U.S. Army War College Press

CHINA'S INTERESTS AND GOALS
IN THE ARCTIC:
IMPLICATIONS FOR THE UNITED STATES

Elizabeth Wishnick

March 2017

*****

*****

The author would like to thank Kamila Kolodynska for her excellent research assistance and Samuel Robertson for his expert editing. The author is also grateful to the Chinese scholars, and U.S. officials and scholars who shared their insights with her.

FOREWORD

Although China is not an Arctic state, Chinese officials are taking great pains to demonstrate its intrinsic interests in the Arctic region. As China's global role has grown, it is not surprising that Chinese leaders should seek to take advantage of economic opportunities afforded by the melting Arctic ice, and they are preparing to confront the environmental consequences of Arctic climate change. At this stage, the Chinese leadership has yet to issue an Arctic strategy, although Chinese experts continue to debate their country's interests and goals in the Arctic. U.S.-China relations in the Arctic have thus far been cooperative, but China's growing economic and political ties with Arctic states bear scrutiny, especially in the context of heightened tensions between Russia, China's strategic partner, and the North Atlantic Treaty Organization (NATO).

Dr. Wishnick, an expert on China and Russia, who has previously contributed monographs to the Strategic Studies Institute (SSI) on U.S. policy and regional security in Eurasia (*Russia, China, and the United States in Central Asia: Prospects for Great Power Competition and Cooperation in the Shadow of the Georgian Crisis,* 2009; *Strategic Consequences of the Iraq War: U.S. Security Interests in Central Asia Reassessed,* 2004; *Growing U.S. Security Interests in Central Asia,* 2002), examines China's diplomacy toward the Arctic states and the prospects for cooperation or conflict between China and the United States in the Arctic. Indeed, China finds itself at a relative disadvantage in the Arctic and consequently has opted for multilateral approaches that make use of its observer status in the region's lone governance institution, the Arctic Council, a sharp contrast from the country's typical preference for bilateral diplomatic mechanisms that take advantage of its superior economic leverage.

In this Letort Paper, Dr. Wishnick highlights that China is playing a long game in the Arctic and is deftly building partnerships with a wide range of partners in the region to make sure that China will have a voice on Arctic affairs in the future. She argues that conflict has not characterized the Arctic region thus far and that China's growing interest in the region is unlikely to change that. Nonetheless, she highlights that China's actions in the Arctic have a great impact on U.S. global priorities, including: freedom of navigation; the economic and political stability of Europe; and strategic concerns in other areas, such as the role of Russia in Europe and of China in the South China Sea.

Although cooperation has largely characterized the interaction among Arctic states in the post-Cold War period, she further points out the danger that the conflict over European security issues between Russia and NATO will spill over into the Arctic. Russia has the longest coastline in the Arctic Circle and needs to invest in infrastructure to develop it. Dr. Wishnick argues that discussion of an "icebreaker gap" is not very helpful — it would make no sense for the United States to compete with Russia, which has an extensive Arctic coastline, in the deployment of icebreakers, nor do we have the resources or rationale to do so. This Letort Paper concludes with a discussion of the mismatch between available security governance mechanisms in the Arctic and current threats, and makes suggestions for new approaches to address current Arctic security issues.

Douglas C. Lovelace

DOUGLAS C. LOVELACE, JR.
Director
Strategic Studies Institute and
    U.S. Army War College Press

ABOUT THE AUTHOR

ELIZABETH WISHNICK is a professor of political science at Montclair State University and a Senior Research Scholar at the Weatherhead East Asian Institute, Columbia University. Her latest book project, *China's Risk: Oil, Water, Food and Regional Security* (forthcoming from Columbia University Press), addresses the security and foreign policy consequences for the Asia-Pacific region of oil, water, and food risks in China. Dr. Wishnick also is currently writing several articles about contemporary Sino-Russian relations. She is the author of *Mending Fences: The Evolution of Moscow's China Policy from Brezhnev to Yeltsin* (Seattle: University of Washington Press, 2001 and 2015). Dr. Wishnick was a Public Policy Scholar at the Woodrow Wilson International Center for Scholars in Spring 2012, and a fellow at Columbia's Center for International Conflict Resolution from 2011-2013. She was previously a Fulbright scholar in Hong Kong (2002-2003), and a visiting scholar at the Academia Sinica in Taiwan, the Hoover Institution, and the Davis Center at Harvard University. She received a Ph.D. in political science from Columbia University, an M.A. in Russian and East European studies from Yale University, and a B.A. from Barnard College.

SUMMARY

This Letort Paper examines the geopolitical implications of China's growing involvement in the Arctic for U.S. interests. First, the evolution of U.S. Arctic strategy, including its political and military components, is discussed. Next, China's interests and goals in the Arctic are addressed. A third section examines the Arctic in China's relations with Canada, Russia, and the Nordic states. This Letort Paper then evaluates the consequences of China's expanding Arctic presence for U.S. security interests and concludes with policy recommendations.

CHINA'S INTERESTS AND GOALS IN THE ARCTIC: IMPLICATIONS FOR THE UNITED STATES

INTRODUCTION

As China becomes a global power, it is not surprising that it is turning its attention to the Arctic, one of the last great frontiers, to take advantage of new economic opportunities and join in global efforts to understand the implications of climate change in the region. Indeed, Chinese experts take great pains to demonstrate their country's longstanding interest in the Arctic, dating to 1925 when China signed the Svalbard Treaty, which establishes Norwegian sovereignty over Svalbard (islands formerly called Spitzbergen) as a well as a regime to demilitarize, protect and provide access to the area's resources. In 2004, China acquired its first foothold in the Arctic when it opened its first Arctic research facility, the Yellow River Station, on Svalbard. To Arctic states, however, China is a powerful outsider and China's growing involvement in the region has attracted some of the greatest scrutiny of all the non-Arctic states seeking to play a role there.

The Chinese government has yet to release its Arctic strategy, though some recent official statements have outlined Chinese positions on a number of economic, political, and environmental issues. Chinese analysts have been debating what China's role in the Arctic should be and how best to categorize China's position so as to enable it to take advantage of opportunities and participate in Arctic affairs. However, some provocative statements by prominent

Chinese officials that identify China as a "near-Arctic state" and refer to the resources in the region as the "common heritage of mankind" have dominated the international media discussion of China and the Arctic.

At the same time that China has been elaborating its position on the Arctic, developing its capacity to participate in Arctic economic and scientific affairs, and activating its Arctic diplomacy, the United States has been refining its own Arctic strategy largely in response to threats and opportunities opened up by changes in the Arctic environment. Although the United States and China have largely had cooperative relations in the Arctic, China's emergence as an Arctic player takes place at a time of rising tension between China and the United States over freedom of navigation in the South China Sea, China's emergence as a global naval power, and a deepening Sino-Russian partnership, involving some cooperative projects in the Arctic. Moreover, the worsening international climate in the wake of the conflict in Ukraine and rising tensions between Russia and the North Atlantic Treaty Organization (NATO) threaten to remilitarize the Arctic, which, since the end of the Cold War, regional stakeholders have sought to develop into a zone of peaceful cooperation.

This Letort Paper examines the geopolitical implications of China's growing involvement in the Arctic for U.S. interests. First, the evolution of U.S. Arctic strategy is discussed, including its political and military components. Next, China's interests and goals in the Arctic are addressed. A third section examines the Arctic in China's relations with Canada, Russia, and the Nordic states. This Letort Paper then evaluates the consequences of China's expanding Arctic presence for U.S. security interests and concludes with policy recommendations.

BACKGROUND

According to the U.S. Geological Survey (USGS), the Arctic—areas north of the Arctic Circle (lat. 66.56° N) amounting to 6 percent of the world's landmass, including parts of Alaska—holds the world's largest remaining supplies of unexplored oil and gas, mostly offshore. Potentially there could be as much as 90 billion barrels of oil, 1,669 trillion cubic feet of natural gas, and 44 billion barrels of liquid natural gas (LNG).[1] This identifies, according to the USGS mean estimate, that 13 percent of the world's undiscovered oil, 30 percent of undiscovered gas, and 20 percent of the world's LNG can be found in the Arctic.[2] Arctic areas also contain vast quantities of minerals, including gold, platinum, lead, iron, zinc, uranium, and rare earths.

Because the Arctic ice has been melting at a faster pace in recent years, these resources may be recoverable, once states acquire the necessary infrastructure and technological capacities to explore in these areas. According to the U.S. Environmental Protection Agency, 2012 saw the lowest extent of Arctic ice coverage recorded, 49% below the 1979-2000 average for that month.[3] See Figure 1 for a comparison of the sea ice extent during the typical minimum-level month of 1979 versus 2014, and Figure 2 for a depiction of the 2012 low ice compared to the median line.

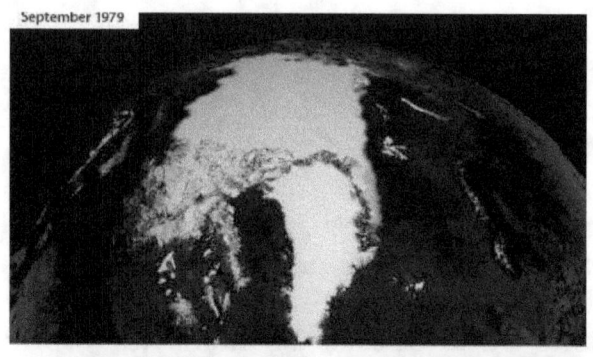

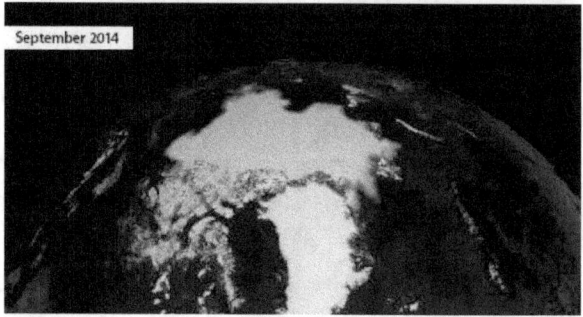

Figure 1. Dwindling Arctic Sea Ice.[4]

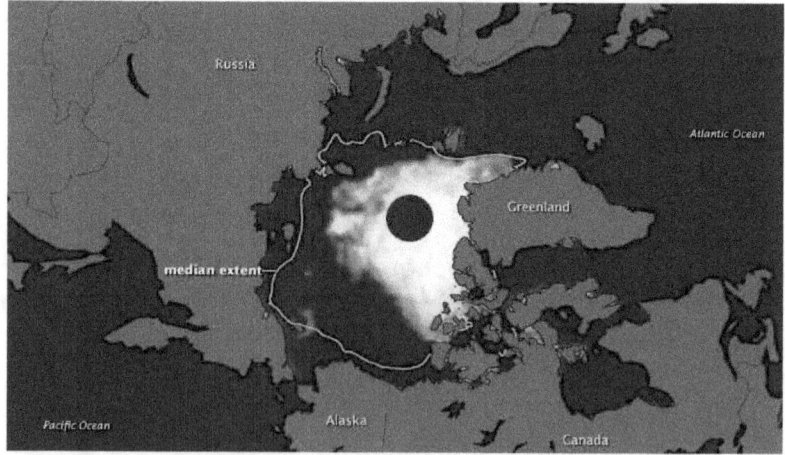

Figure 2. National Aeronautics and Space Administration (NASA) Special Sensor Microwave Imager/Sounder (SSMIS) View of the 2012 Record Low Arctic Ice.[5]

The National Snow and Ice Data Center reports that the ice extent for November 2016 was the lowest on record, based on satellite observations (see Figure 3).[6]

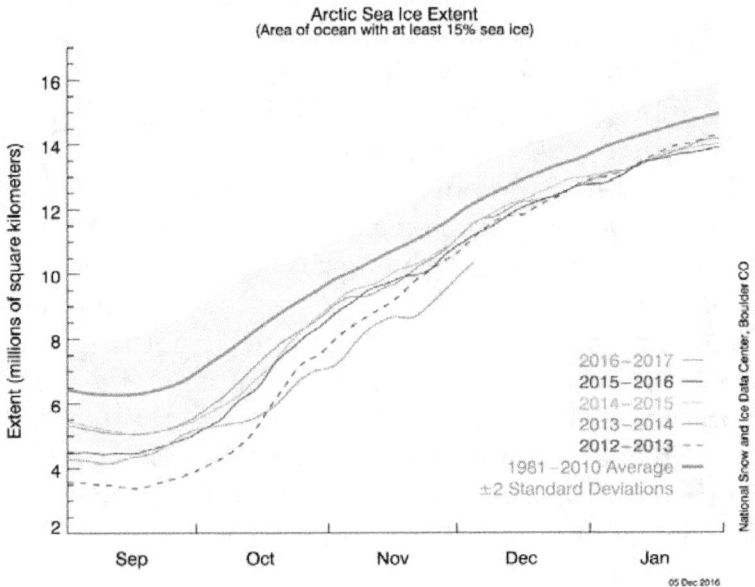

Figure 3. The National Snow and Ice Data Center Sees a Record Low Ice Cover For 2016.[7]

Less Arctic ice in the summer months means more opportunities for shipping and tourism. Arctic cruises are now an option and the Crystal Line, an American luxury cruise outfit, made its first 32-day cruise along the Northwest Passage in August-September 2016, with 1,070 passengers and 655 crew aboard. Although the cabin price per person ranged from $22,000 to $46,000 per person, the cruise reportedly sold out within a week.[8] This cruise involved 3 years of planning for the company, as well as the coordinated cooperation of U.S. and Canadian Coast Guard authorities to address potential maritime safety issues in the still uncertain environment of the Northwest Passage, which, though more navigable in summer months than a decade ago, still lacks sufficient infrastructure for widespread commercial use.

According to the U.S. Coast Guard, the expansion of commercial activity will pose substantial logistical challenges in case of a shipping accident or oil spill. Barrow, Alaska, the only major U.S. city in the Arctic Circle, has only limited air and sea access. Dutch Harbor, the only deepwater port the United States has, is in the Aleutian Islands, more than 1,200 miles away from Barrow. There are limited airports, roads, and communications infrastructure in the U.S. Arctic. At present, the United States has only two functioning icebreakers: the recently overhauled *Polar Star*, a heavy icebreaker; and the *Healy*, a medium icebreaker, which is mainly used to support scientific research.[9]

	Total all types, in inventory (+under construction + planned)	In inventory, government owned or operated			In inventory, privately owned and operated		
		45,000 or more BHP	20,000 to 44,999 BHP	10,000 to 19,999 BHP	45,000 or more BHP	20,000 to 44,999 BHP	10,000 to 19,999 BHP
Russia	41 (+ 5 + 6)	6 (all nuclear powered; 4 operational)	6	7		13	9
Finland	7 (+0 +1)					6	1
Sweden	6		4				2
Canada	6 (+0 +1)		2	4			
United States	5 (+0 +1)	2 (*Polar Star* and *Polar Sea*—Polar Sea not operational)	1 (*Healy*)			1 (*Aiviq*— built for Shell Oil)	1 (*Palmer*)
China	1 (+0 +1)			1			

Table 1. Selected World-Wide Icebreaker Capability, Data from May 21, 2015.[10]

Shipping companies also see opportunity in the reduced summer ice cover to lower their shipping times by using the two trans-Arctic shipping routes: the Northwest Passage in North America, and the Northern Sea Route (NSR) in Europe. In the short term, the unpredictability of Arctic ice floes makes these routes impractical for container shipping, because they require an exact timeframe, but are better suited to bulk shipping. A third route, the transpolar route, is not yet navigable. Destinational shipping, in support of resource extraction in the Arctic, will also increase as economic activity increases in the region. Nonetheless, despite the current changeable conditions, shipping through the Bering Straits has doubled since 2007 and there are now approximately 400 transit shipments annually.[11] However, shipping along the full length of the Northwest Passage remains modest, approximately 75 vessels from 2011-2015 traveled this route, compared to over 200 for the NSR during the same period (see Figure 4).[12] The NSR reduces travel time from Asia to Europe, versus the Suez Canal route, by about 10 days; and the Northwest Passage is 4 days shorter than the Panama Canal route.

Arctic Sea Route Navigability

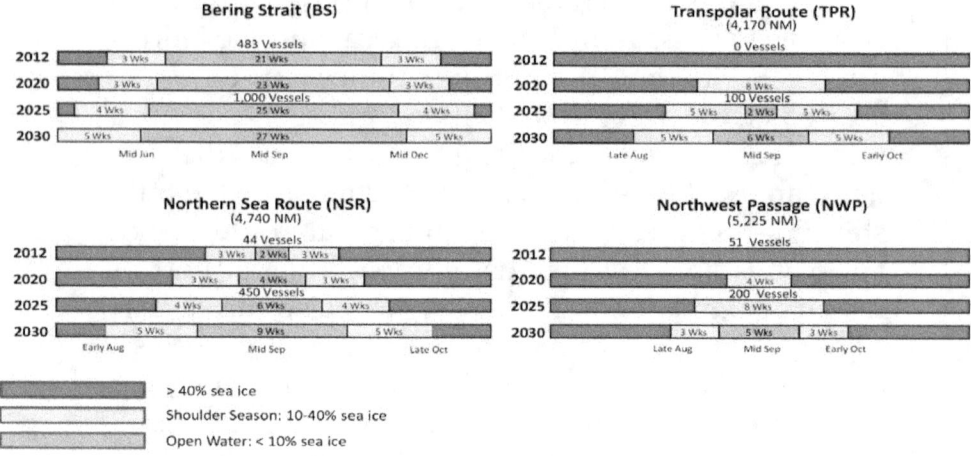

Figure 4. U.S. Navy Estimates of the Likelihood of Open Water Navigation in the Arctic.[13]

According to the U.S. Navy, the NSR will see the greatest expansion of shipping in the near term and mid term. By 2020, the Navy predicts that the Transpolar Route will be navigable for short periods; and by 2030, there will be significant opportunities for shipping along all three routes (see Figure 5).[14]

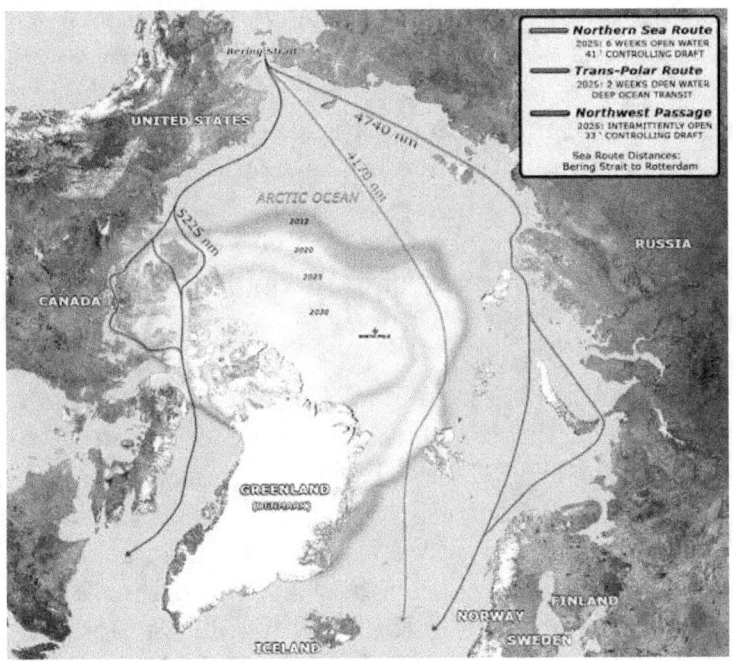

Figure 5. U.S. Navy Estimates of the Navigability of the Polar Routes.[15]

Nonetheless, Arctic areas are highly vulnerable to the effects of climate change, and changes to date (receding ice, rising seawater, warming water temperatures, and the impacting effect on animals and fish) have already altered the hunting practices of indigenous communities and forced some to relocate. Moreover, the effects of climate change in the Arctic region itself, by releasing methane from melting permafrost, may compound the impact of climate changes in areas south of the Arctic.[16] The unusual melting in Northwest Greenland in 2015 led to a phenomenon known as Arctic amplification, according to which the disproportionate impact of climate change on the Arctic led to additional ice melting, which left more open water that in turn absorbed additional heat from the sun, which led to even greater warming.[17] These trends heighten the importance of scientific research on processes of climate change in the Arctic for regional and non-Arctic states alike.

Arctic governance first evolved as a result of environmental concerns and geopolitical changes in the late 1980s. At the time, the Arctic was the only land border between NATO countries and the Soviet Union, while U.S. and Soviet submarines engaged in tense cat and mouse games under the region's frozen waters. The 1986 Chernobyl nuclear accident and the Soviet Union's dumping of radioactive waste in the Kola Peninsula and White Sea heightened concern in Europe about transboundary pollution. Finland, which borders on the Kola peninsula, responded by engaging its Arctic neighbors in a diplomatic effort to cooperate in environmental protection, an effort which culminated in a 1991 meeting where the eight Arctic states signed a Declaration on the Protection of the Arctic Environment and agreed to the Arctic Environmental Protection Strategy. The international climate was propitious for such an initiative, as then-Soviet leader Mikhail Gorbachev had called for the Arctic to become a "zone of peace" in a 1987 speech in Murmansk, located in the Russian Arctic. Former Canadian Prime Minister Brian Mulroney responded to Gorbachev's appeal 2 years later with a proposal for the Arctic Council that came into being in 1996 with Canada as its first chairman.[18]

U.S. POLICY TOWARD THE ARCTIC

In 1971, the National Security Decision Memorandum 144 first defined three broad U.S. goals in the Arctic: 1) minimizing environmental damage; 2) enhancing international cooperation; and, 3) protecting the security of the region, including freedom of navigation and airspace.[19] The Reagan administration's 1983 National Security Decision Directive added scientific research as a fourth goal of U.S. Arctic policy;[20] and the 1984 Arctic Research and Policy Act established a commission to develop U.S. Arctic research. Former U.S. President Bill Clinton's Presidential Decision Directive (PDD)/National Security Council (NSC)-26 issued in 1994, and the Bush administration's final presidential directive of January 9, 2009, the National Security Presidential Directive (NSPD)-66, further elaborated the goals of the U.S. Arctic policy. According to the 2009 document, U.S. Arctic policy aimed to:

1. Meet national security and homeland security needs relevant to the Arctic region;
2. Protect the Arctic environment and conserve its biological resources;
3. Ensure that natural resource management and economic development in the region are environmentally sustainable;
4. Strengthen institutions for cooperation among the eight Arctic nations . . . ;
5. Involve indigenous communities in decisions that affect them; and,
6. Enhance scientific monitoring and research.[21]

According to NSPD-66, U.S. national security and homeland security interests in the Arctic include:
- Maintaining missile defense and early warning systems;

11

- Deploying sea and air systems for strategic sealift (i.e. transport of military personnel and equipment);
- Pursuing strategic deterrence;
- Asserting a stronger maritime presence and enhancing maritime security operations;
- Ensuring freedom of navigation (especially transit passage) and overflight; and,
- Preventing terrorist attacks and mitigating criminal or hostile acts.[22]

To carry out U.S. national security and homeland security interests, NSPD-66 asks U.S. agencies to:

1. Develop greater capabilities and capacity . . . to protect [U.S. Arctic borders and interests];
2. Increase Arctic maritime domain awareness . . . to protect [trade, infrastructure, and resources];
3. Preserve the global mobility of United States military and civilian vessels and aircraft [in the Arctic];
4. Project a sovereign United States maritime presence in the Arctic in support of . . . United States interests; and,
5. Encourage the peaceful resolution of disputes.[23]

The 2010 U.S. *National Security Strategy*, the first issued after former President Barack Obama took office, depicted the United States as:

an Arctic Nation with broad and fundamental interests in the Arctic region, where we seek to meet our national security needs, protect the environment, responsibly manage resources, account for indigenous communities, support scientific research, and strengthen international cooperation on a wide range of issues.[24]

In April 2011, one of the first steps the Obama administration took regarding Arctic security was to consolidate the military command over U.S. Arctic territories (including Alaska) and waters under the U.S. Northern Command (NORTHCOM). Previously, NORTHCOM had shared this responsibility with the European Command and the Pacific Command (PACOM).[25]

In May 2013, the Obama administration's Arctic policy expanded on the Bush administration's Arctic directive in the *National Strategy for the Arctic Region*.[26] The 2013 national strategy reflects changes in the Arctic environment that led to growing interest in trade and resource development in the region by Arctic and non-Arctic states. The document includes discussion of the role of the Arctic in ensuring U.S. energy security, the role of the Arctic Council and International Maritime Organization (the United Nations [UN] agency focusing on maritime safety and security) in Arctic governance, and the need to discuss Arctic issues with all interested parties, including non-Arctic states and nonstate actors.

The U.S. Coast Guard, the maritime arm of the Department of Homeland Security, also outlined its vision for the Arctic region in May 2013, which highlights the importance of modernizing governance, broadening partnerships, and improving domain awareness.[27] The latter involves enhancing communication and information sharing, improving information gathering and intelligence, and achieving an effective maritime presence in the Arctic region.[28]

After the Obama administration unveiled its Arctic strategy, the U.S. military followed suit. In November 2013, the U.S. Department of Defense (DoD) outlined its strategy for the Arctic as "a secure and stable region where U.S. national interests are safeguarded, the U.S. homeland is protected, and nations work cooperatively to address challenges."[29] This would entail ensuring environmental and human security, supporting safety, promoting defense cooperation, and preparing to respond to challenges and contingencies, preferably in conjunction with allies and partners in the region. The strategy notes the considerable uncertainties involved in ensuring the security and stability of the Arctic as well as the potential for miscommunication and inflammatory rhetoric to exacerbate tensions over sovereignty and other interstate issues.

In January 2014, the Obama administration outlined the *Implementation Plan for the National Strategy for the Arctic Region*. In the security area, the plan largely took a long-term approach, advocating a range of studies on projected maritime activity in the region, assessing telecommunications infrastructure, evaluating the use of unmanned aerial systems (UAS) to enhance maritime domain awareness, sustaining capabilities to operate in Arctic waters, and encouraging the use of renewable energy. The only concrete plans involved completing ongoing aviation infrastructure improvements and continuing maritime exercises in the region.[30] After Alaska Senator Lisa Murkowski criticized the implementation plan for lacking a "real path to action," Secretary of State John Kerry appointed Admiral Robert J. Papp, Jr., U.S. Coast Guard (Ret.) as the Special Representative for the Arctic in July of 2014.[31]

In February 2014, the U.S. Navy issued a report outlining its objectives in the Arctic to 2030. These include:

- *Ensure United States Arctic sovereignty and provide homeland defense;*
- *Providing ready naval forces* to respond to crisis and contingencies;

- *Preserve freedom of the seas*; and,
- *Promote partnerships* within the United States Government and with international allies and partners [emphasis in original].[32]

The Navy's key missions, such as maritime security, protection of sea lanes, and access to maritime resources, power projection, and search and rescue, will also be important in defining its role in the Arctic in coming decades.[33]

The United States began its second 2-year term as Chairman of the Arctic Council, the intergovernmental organization of Arctic states, on April 24, 2015.[34] As Chairman, the U.S. focuses on three priorities: "Improving Economic & Living Conditions for Arctic Communities; Arctic Ocean Safety, Security & Stewardship; [and] Addressing the Impacts of Climate Change."[35] The Arctic Council was established in 1996 and its permanent membership includes eight Arctic states—Canada, Denmark (including Greenland and the Faroe Islands), Finland, Iceland, Norway, Sweden, Russia, and the United States—and six permanent participants, which are groups representing Arctic indigenous peoples.[36]

The priorities of the United States as Chairman of the Arctic Council reflect the organization's emphasis on environmental, scientific, and economic cooperation. This organization has never sought to play a role in security governance, and stakeholders tend to view security concerns as intrusions in its governance. In fact, the Ottawa Declaration—the founding document for the forum—specifically states, "The Arctic Council should not deal with matters related to military security."[37] As a consequence, the Arctic Council's agreements on maritime security, such as the 2009

15

Agreement on Aeronautical and Maritime Search and Rescue in the Arctic, and the 2011 Agreement on Cooperation on Marine Oil Preparedness and Response in the Arctic, focus on coordination among the Coast Guards of Arctic states rather than the involvement of their militaries.[38] Nonetheless, the United States mentions Arctic Ocean security in its priorities for its current period of chairmanship, which reflects its greater emphasis on security than many other Arctic states. According to Rear Admiral Nils Wang, Commandant of the Danish Royal Defence Academy, the U.S. priority on freedom of navigation in Arctic waters puts Washington at odds with Canada and Russia, because both assert that what the U.S. considers international straits are their internal waters.[39] Since the United States has yet to ratify the UN Convention on the Law of the Sea (UNCLOS), the U.S. government is unable to assert any territorial claims of its own in the Arctic, though the United States follows UNCLOS as customary law.

With the United States assuming a higher profile role on Arctic Affairs, observers inside and outside government have criticized the Obama administration about its priorities for the region and the resources committed to implement them. Heather Conley, an Arctic expert at the Center for Strategic and International Studies (CSIS), argued in 2014 that the administration lacked a long-term vision for the Arctic and the budgetary allocation to develop needed infrastructure in the region.[40] Senators Murkowski (R-Alaska) and Angus King (I-Maine) created the Senate Arctic Caucus in March 2015 to develop legislation for improved Arctic infrastructure and to better focus attention on regional concerns.[41] The conference report on the fiscal year (FY) 2016 National Defense Authorization Act also requires the Secretary of Defense to update the U.S. Arctic strategy (last issued in 2013) within 1 year of the legislation's passage,[42] i.e. by November 25, 2016; however, by January 1, 2017, a new strategy had yet to be released to the public.

The Obama administration had sought to refocus efforts on the region. In January 2015, the Obama administration issued an Executive Order for Enhancing Coordination of National Efforts in the Arctic, which created an Arctic Executive Steering Committee for the U.S. government, housed in the White House Office. Headed by Mark Brzezinski, a former U.S. Ambassador to Sweden and NSC Director for Russia and Eurasia, the new committee was designed to better coordinate Arctic efforts throughout the government, improve engagement with Alaskan and Arctic native communities, as well as support the U.S. role as Chairman of the Arctic Council in 2015-17.[43]

Former President Obama expressed a particular interest in Arctic issues and visited Alaska in early September 2015—including a stop in Kotzebue, the first presidential visit to a U.S. city in the Arctic Circle—to call attention to the effects of climate change on the state.[44] The former President addressed a State Department conference on Global Leadership in the Arctic: Cooperation, Innovation, Engagement, and Resilience (called the GLACIER conference), and the White House dedicated a webpage to the presidential visit, which includes a series of podcasts detailing Obama's personal reflections on the threat climate change poses to Alaska.[45]

The visit was notable for several reasons. During his visit to Alaska, Obama announced the administration's commitment to acquiring a new heavy icebreaker and building additional icebreaker capacity. The Coast Guard estimates that three heavy ice-breakers and three medium icebreakers would be needed to meet its mission demands in polar regions.[46] The President explained that the U.S. icebreaker fleet has declined since the end of World War II, when we had seven, to three today under U.S. Coast Guard command (with only two fully operational, and only one of those a heavy icebreaker). The President noted that Russia, by comparison, has more than forty ice-breakers with at least another eleven planned.[47]

In March 2016, the White House Arctic Executive Steering Committee issued a progress report on the implementation of the 2013 Arctic strategy as well as a 5-year implementation plan. Following the 2013 Arctic strategy, the 2016 progress report emphasizes the priority of advancing U.S. security interests. This goal is to be implemented by improving domain awareness (through various mapping efforts in the Arctic), up-grading infrastructure in anticipation of greater access to the Arctic, highlighting freedom of the seas, and en-hancing energy security in a sustainable and safe way. Although expanding the U.S. icebreaker capability is a primary concern, the lack of an Arctic deepwater port is another consideration, and the Army Corps of Engi-neers was investigating the merits of such a facility for Nome, Alaska. A 2011 Naval War College simulation of an Arctic Operation concluded:

> the U.S. Navy does not have the means to support sus-tained operations in the Arctic. This was due primar-ily to the lack of appropriate ship types to operate in or near Arctic ice, the lack of support facilities in the Arctic, and the lack of sufficient or capable logistics connectors to account for the long logistics distances and lack of facilities.[48]

With the decline in world oil prices, however, Shell decided in 2015 to abandon an offshore oil venture off the coast of Alaska, which has altered the cost-benefit analysis for a deepwater port, at least for the short-term needs of the energy sector. In the March 2016 Senate hearings, Assistant Secretary of the Army for Civil Works Jo-Ellen Darcy explained that, despite the cancellation of the Shell project, the construction of the deepwater port in Nome may be revisited, for example, to house the Coast Guard's future new ice-breaker.[49]

As the discussion in a November 2015 congressional hearing on the Arctic attests, broader security considerations have been encroaching of late on policy discussions of U.S. interests in the Arctic. Members of Congress repeatedly questioned Admiral Papp, Rear Admiral Gallaudet of the U.S. Navy, and Vice Admiral Charles Michel of the U.S. Coast Guard on the Russian military buildup in the Arctic, linked Chinese access to the Arctic to their behavior in the South China Sea, and highlighted the possibility of joint Sino-Russian activity in the Arctic.[50] While noting that Russian actions in Ukraine "have complicated our efforts in the Arctic" and criticizing Russian aggression there, Admiral Papp emphasized that the United States and other countries have a successful record of working with Russia on Arctic issues of mutual interest during previous periods of crisis.[51] He further explained, in response to questions, that what is portrayed as a "militarization" of the Arctic can be better understood as a reasonable effort to secure a lengthy waterway — accounting for half the Arctic — that faces increasing traffic.[52] Rear Admiral Gallaudet added, "in our opinion their intention is primarily economic development and we feel no threat in the Arctic by the Russians."[53]

Michel further explained that the U.S. Coast Guard has a good working relationship with the Russian Border Guards on fisheries and search and rescue issues. Both Gallaudet and Michel also presented China's developing role in the Arctic in a positive light. Michel highlighted the cooperative relations between the Chinese and U.S. Coast Guards, while Gallaudet pointed out that the September 2015 innocent passage voyage by the Chinese People's Liberation Army Navy (PLAN) in U.S. Arctic waters "made a very good case for us to point to what they are doing in the South China Sea, and show that that was inconsistent and not following the rule of law."[54]

U.S. FORCES AND MILITARY COOPERATION IN THE ARCTIC

The U.S. military presence in the Arctic dates from World War II. A year after the German occupation of Denmark on June 7, 1941, U.S. Secretary of State Cordell Hull agreed with the Danish Ambassador to assume responsibility for the security of Greenland. This led to the development of weather stations in various locations there, which proved instrumental in Allied planning for the Normandy invasion of 1944. After the war, the United States and Denmark established the Thule Air Base in western Greenland where 600 personnel (from the United States, Denmark, Greenland, and Canada) provide missile early warning, satellite command and control, and space surveillance capabilities.[55] The Alaskan Command (ALCOM) was created in 1947 in response to lessons learned from World War II, particularly the need for command unity, highlighted in the challenges U.S. forces faced in battles with the Japanese on the Aleutian Islands.

Responsibility for Alaska's defense remained split among the services until a 1987 exercise highlighted the merits of unified defense for Alaska, which then moved to PACOM with the exception of air defense. Alaska NORAD, a component of the North American Aerospace Defense (NORAD), the U.S.-Canada cooperation effort set up during World War II that went on to play a key role during the Cold War in missile defense, is responsible for air security in Alaska.[56]

The end of the Cold War, the September 11, 2001 (9/11), terrorist attacks, U.S. budgetary constraints, and changes in U.S. and NATO relations with Russia have led to further reevaluations of the U.S. military presence in the Arctic.[57] After the 9/11 terrorist attacks, NORTHCOM was created and took over responsibility for Alaska's land and sea defense. With the more rapid melting of Arctic ice in the 2000s, the United States has been confronting the need to secure an entirely new coastline to enable the protection of its first new ocean since the 19th century.[58] The reassignment of responsibility for Alaska's defense reflects this change. On October 27, 2014, ALCOM was transferred from PACOM to NORTHCOM.[59]

Shifting priorities, namely the growing threats facing the United States in the Middle East and budgetary constraints, led to the closure in 2006 of the U.S. Naval air base in Keflavik in southwest Iceland, created in 1951 to monitor Soviet submarine traffic. In light of recent U.S. and NATO tensions with Russia, and against the background of closer economic ties between an economically weakened Iceland and China, the U.S. Navy requested funds in its 2017 budget request to upgrade an aircraft hangar at the base to support increased U.S. patrols for Russian submarines.[60] Similarly, in July 2015, the U.S. Army's 4th Brigade Combat Team, 25th

Infantry Division, which operates from Joint Base El-mendorf-Richardson in Alaska, was supposed to lose 3,000 Soldiers — from 4,000 to approximately 1,050 — as a result of defense budget cuts. By March 2016, Acting Army Secretary Patrick Murphy was arguing that the brigade was needed and cited Russian aggression, as well as threats from North Korea and the Islamic State of Iraq and the Levant (ISIL), to justify sparing the 25th Infantry from budget cuts.[61] The 4th Brigade is the Army's only extreme cold weather brigade and is an airborne unit, and therefore, is a key component for rapid response needs in the Arctic and the Asia-Pacific region.[62] In August 2016, the 4th Brigade participated in Arctic Anvil 2016, the largest Arctic Army training exercise in 15 years, involving 8,000 personnel largely from the U.S. Army, but also including some Canadian forces.[63]

Meanwhile, in March 2016, the U.S. Navy, led by the Submarine Forces Command, staged its first Arctic ice exercise (ICEX) since 2014. Although Navy officials downplayed any connection between ICEX 2016 and concerns about Russian policies or military deployments, the 2014 ICEX involved a simulated torpedo firing against a simulated Akula-class Russian sub.[64] While the 2014 ICEX was scheduled prior to Russian actions in Crimea, the exercise, involving British, Canadian, and Norwegian forces, was meant to reassure NATO allies, especially in the Baltic region. Nonetheless, these exercises are now biannual and much less frequent than during the Cold War, when they occurred three times per year.[65]

Prior to the Russian conflict with Ukraine, NATO was opposed to building up military capabilities in the Arctic, and NATO Secretary General Anders Rasmussen urged states to cooperate in the region.[66] Similarly, a 2015 U.S. Government Accountability Office

(GAO) report noted that the DoD expected to play a supporting role in the Arctic given the perceived low level of threat and the willingness thus far of Arctic states to cooperate within the framework of the Arctic Council and UNCLOS. Thus, the DoD may assist the Coast Guard with search and rescue missions or the Federal Emergency Management Agency (FEMA) with disaster response.[67] Although disputes with other Arctic states or non-Arctic stakeholders over fisheries or maritime boundaries could lead to conflict, the 2013 DoD Strategy warns of the danger of militarizing the Arctic, lest this lead to mistrust and miscommunication. The 2013 Strategy states that there:

> is some risk that the perception that the Arctic is being militarized may lead to an 'arms race mentality' that could lead to a breakdown of existing cooperative approaches to shared challenges.[68]

The 2015 GAO report goes on to discuss the DoD's involvement in multilateral security, such as the Arctic Security Forces Roundtable (co-hosted by the United States and Norway) and the Northern Chiefs of Defense conference, as an example of regional capacity to address Arctic security issues.[69] However, the conflict between the United States, the European Union (EU), and Russia over Ukraine has led to the cancellation of the latter for the past 3 years and the former has been held without Russian participation. According to Andreas Østhagen of the Norwegian Institute for Defence Studies and the Arctic Institute, "organizing Arctic security without Russia defeats some of the main purpose why such venues were created."[70] He further notes that while conflict over the Arctic may be unlikely, a deterioration in relations among regional states may lead to conflict within the Arctic for reasons not connected to the region.[71]

CHINA'S INTERESTS AND GOALS IN THE ARCTIC

China's increasing activity in the Arctic creates a new area of uncertainty. The Chinese government has yet to articulate an Arctic strategy and has been treading cautiously and proceeding incrementally. In recent years, China has been expanding its trade and investment ties with northern European states and improving its polar research capacity.[72] After several attempts, in 2013, China successfully became an observer in the Arctic Council, which Chinese officials interpreted as recognition of their country's legitimate interests in the Arctic. Nonetheless, China's funding for its Arctic activities remains relatively modest: 20 percent of $60 million is allocated for all Polar activities.[73] China has been engaged in a 5-year assessment (2012-2016) of polar resources and governance, which aims to increase China's status and influence in polar affairs to better protect its polar rights. These rights refer to its scientific and economic activities at Svalbard, Norway (where it has had a research station since 2004), observer status in Arctic Council, access to Arctic seas and air rights, participation in international governance of Arctic matters, and bidding for mineral rights.[74]

To some extent, the ambiguity in Chinese official positions may be intentional—Chinese officials highlight the need for cooperation with foreign partners, but use the Arctic issue to speak to nationalist interests at home who fear Chinese exclusion and seek its rightful place in the world.[75] However, some of the language used by Chinese commentators, defining China as a near-Arctic state and a stakeholder in the region, and referring to its resources as the common heritage of mankind, has raised fears about Chinese intentions. Article 32 of the July 1, 2015 Chinese National Security Law outlines the government's role:

> in the peaceful exploration and use of . . . international seabed areas and polar regions, increasing capacity for safe passage, scientific investigation, development and exploitation; strengthening international cooperation, and preserving the security of our nation's activities and assets in. . . . seabed areas and polar regions, and other interests.[76]

While many Chinese analysts argue that China needs a strategy and should outline one to avoid missing out on opportunities, others argue that the lack of a strategy will help calm fears in the region about China's intentions.

Observers inside and outside China report that China's Ministry of Foreign Affairs coordinates its overall Arctic policy, though they disagree over the balance of power within the Arctic *xitong* (grouping of bureaucracies), with some arguing that the State Oceanic Administration and state-owned energy and shipping companies are seeking greater input.[77] In October 2015, Foreign Minister Wang Yi issued a video message to the Arctic Circle Assembly, an open forum devoted to Arctic issues, in which he outlined respect, cooperation, and win-win results as the guiding principles of China's Arctic diplomacy. Regarding respect, Wang explained:

> Respect provides the important basis for China's participation in Arctic affairs. China respects Arctic coun-

tries' sovereignty, sovereign rights, and jurisdiction in the Arctic, and the traditions and culture of Arctic indigenous people. China also believes that the legitimate concerns of non-Arctic countries and the rights they enjoy under international law in the Arctic and the collective interests of the international community should be respected.[78]

Vice Foreign Minister Zhang Ming amplified the Foreign Minister's remarks on a panel at the Arctic Assembly "mandated" by Chinese President Xi Jinping to present China's policies, projects, and vision for the Arctic in response to an invitation by Iceland's President, Ólafur Ragnar Grímsson.[79] Zhang began by describing China as a "near-Arctic state" and "major stakeholder in the Arctic," because of the direct impact that the Arctic's environment and resources have on the environment, climate, agriculture, shipping, trade, and socio-economic development in China.[80] In his remarks, Zhang outlined six key policies that China would follow in the Arctic. The first policy was to explore and understand the Arctic through partnerships between government, academia, business, and social organizations. The second policy revolved around protecting the Arctic and developing the regional sustainability. The third policy outlined the need to respect the "inherent rights" of Arctic states, who have territorial sovereignty, and the culture, traditions, and lifestyles of indigenous peoples. The fourth policy is as follows:

> **Respect the rights of non-Arctic countries** and the overall interests of the international community. The Arctic seas include high seas and international sea-bed areas. Non-Arctic countries have the rights to conduct scientific research, navigation and exploration in the

Arctic under international law and these rights should be respected and upheld. The international community must work together to protect and utilize the Arctic, and in particular to address such global issues as climate change, ecology, environmental protection and shipping. At the same time, **the overall interests of the international community in the Arctic should be respected** [emphasis added].[81]

The fifth policy talked about the need to develop a multi-tiered governance framework at the global, regional, and national levels, and the need to seek mutually beneficial cooperation.

The challenges in the Arctic require joint contribution of **all stakeholders, including the expertise, technology, capital and market that non-Arctic countries** may offer [emphasis added].[82]

And lastly, the sixth policy called for supporting the current governance framework for the Arctic, based on existing international law (UN Charter, UNCLOS, Svalbard Treaty, etc.). In light of this framework, "Arctic and non-Arctic countries are **entitled to their rights** and also shoulder obligations under international law [emphasis added]."[83] China recognizes the role of organizations such as the Arctic Council and the International Maritime Organization in Arctic governance.

U.S. and European scholars' studies identify China's objectives as: 1) access to mineral, fish, and energy resources; 2) new trade routes that shorten shipping time and provide an alternative to the Malacca Straits; 3) interest in understanding the impact of climate change on the region; 4) scientific interests (China's BeiDou navigational satellite system, space science, weather forecasting); 5) participation in Arctic governance; and, 6) calling attention to rights of non-Arctic states and ensuring that the area that does not fall in sovereign territory of Arctic states remains accessible to all.[84] Western observers also note that Chinese officials are concerned about being denied access to Arctic waterways by Arctic states and seek to internationalize Arctic issues, as opposed to limiting their scope to immediate Arctic states.[85] According to Anne-Marie Brady, Chinese officials aim for an open Arctic—where waters are considered open and international, freedom of navigation prevails, and opportunities for resource exploration and environmental research are open to all.[86]

In the Arctic, however, there is more than principle at stake. Chinese shipping predominantly relies on its own southern ports, and China imports resources from areas south of the equator. Ports located in areas north of Shanghai would benefit most from the distance savings offered by Arctic shipping. However, most of China's trade with Europe requires containers and, at present, Arctic shipping is not ideal for container shipping (since it requires precise delivery dates, which are not possible due to unpredictable weather conditions in the Arctic). Moreover, China's trade with Europe has been declining.[87] Opportunities exist in bulk shipping of natural resources obtained in Arctic Russia, but the shipping opportunities there have thus far mainly gone to Russian and European companies, which have the capacity to work in polar conditions. Although shorter shipping timeframes are often mentioned as a rationale for China's growing involvement in the Arctic, the greatest enthusiasm for Chinese participation appears to come from the government and associated researchers who are more concerned with China's role and its access to Arctic resources, not from Chinese shipping companies.[88]

There has been a lively scholarly discussion about China and the Arctic for some years that informs policymakers, though the views of scholars, while affiliated with government institutions, are diverse and should not be equated with official policy positions.[89] Some Chinese scholars highlight the security rationale for China's interest in the Arctic. They call attention to the importance of maritime security for China and see Arctic routes as an alternative to the Malacca Strait,[90] which they fear provides an opportunity for the United States and its allies to choke Chinese access to needed energy supplies from the Persian Gulf. Other Chinese analysts highlight that the Arctic is situated at the crossroads between the EU, Eurasia, and the United States, which houses a ballistic missile interceptor capability at Fort Greely, Alaska that could potentially be directed against China.[91] A naval analyst noted that access to the Arctic would enable China to break out from Western pressure and emerge on the world stage.[92] Other Chinese scholars view the Arctic as important to establish China as a regional military power and to enhance its soft power.[93] Scholars from China's eastern regions see the Arctic as a way of connecting their areas to the One Belt One Road project and further expanding China's energy and transportation networks.[94]

Citing Sun Tzu, "if you know yourself and know your enemy, you will be victorious,"[95] Chinese scholars point out that in this early stage of China's Arctic involvement, when its interests are viewed with some suspicion, it needs to learn from other states and cooperate with them.[96] Due to what some observers term the "Monroe Doctrine" mentality, Arctic states seek to exclude China and other non-Arctic states from key decisions. For this reason, Chinese experts argue, China needs to make use of existing governance options, such as its observer status in the Arctic Council, and deepen other forms of multilateral cooperation, for example, through the research center on Arctic issues established in Shanghai, and the World Reindeer Herders' Congress.[97]

In their analyses, Chinese experts seek to find ways for their country to pursue its legitimate interests in the Arctic without facing undue restrictions. Many analysts emphasize that China has had longstanding interests and involvement in the region. Similar to historical rationales for sovereignty in the South China Sea, Chinese analysts point to historical precedent; in this case, the Republic of China's signing of the 1925 Svalbard Treaty, to indicate that China's interest in the Arctic is far from new.[98] They also point to China's history of scientific missions in the region.

Moreover, the discussion of how to refer to China in the Arctic ("non-Arctic state," "near-Arctic state," "non-Arctic coastal state," or "Arctic stakeholder") has attracted as much attention within China as outside it. Some Chinese scholars argue that "Arctic stakeholder" is the best descriptor for China's Arctic identity, in that the term situates the country as a legitimate participant rather than an external player and opens the possibility for China to be a responsible and cooperative partner.[99] Some also mention that, based on UNCLOS, the Arctic is a common heritage and should not be dominated by great powers.[100]

Defining China's role in the Arctic represents the first stage in China's Arctic policy, writes Sun Kai, an Arctic scholar at the Ocean University of China. The next phase is to elaborate what China should do in its Arctic diplomacy.[101] Sun Kai highlights climate change and the economy as two areas where China would face few barriers to its Arctic diplomacy, and he argues that China should promote its role in these areas by participating in new approaches to Arctic governance, cooperating widely (with Arctic and non-Arctic states, non-governmental organizations (NGOs), and companies), and engaging in Track 2 dialogue.[102]

Chinese analysts note that Arctic governance is in its infancy and suggest that this provides an opportunity for China to be a rule-maker, for example, to protect its fishing and shipping interests.[103] Others note that since the Arctic Council was established relatively recently, this provides China with an opportunity to socialize other members about China's role, as well as for China to learn more about Arctic governance.[104] China's relatively weak position in the Arctic often comes up in Chinese academic discussions of China's role in the region and, for some analysts, provides the primary short-term rationale for China's active involvement as an observer within the Arctic Council.[105] In the long term, according to some scholars, China's best strategy is to reduce barriers to China's participation by supporting existing laws and green development, while enhancing its own position in the Arctic by building its military, economic, and technological capacity to operate in the area and developing new legal approaches.[106] Some analysts chafe at the limitations involved in observer status in the Arctic Council given China's great power role,[107] while others suggest China should develop new multilateral initiatives for Arctic governance in cooperation with states, such as a global maritime cooperation center that would address Arctic issues.[108]

Chinese scholarly analyses of Arctic politics view geopolitics as well as regional governance as key drivers.[109] Chinese academics and military analysts have discussed the prospect of great power conflict and militarization in the Arctic for some years, and this concern is not specifically a response to more recent U.S.-Russian tensions, though these have magnified or given additional credence to longstanding fears over the spillover of great power competition into the Arctic.[110]

Chinese experts generally advise against their country being drawn into U.S.-Russian military competition in the Arctic, though Yang Zhirong of the PLAN's Naval War College observed that the melting ice reduced the distance between great powers in the region and increased its strategic importance.[111] He noted that both the United States and Russia had a military component to their Arctic strategy and urged China to do the same. This would involve dedicating naval staff to Arctic affairs, as well as information-gathering, developing Arctic-capable equipment, improving communication in the region, making ports of call visits, and more generally to recognize the strategic value of the Arctic. Yang pointed out that had Russia had access to it in 1904, this would have enabled it to direct more resources against Japan.[112]

Chinese experts note that most regional states, including the United States, seek mutually beneficial cooperation. Some Chinese analysts are more suspicious of U.S. aims in the Arctic and urge vigilance,[113] while others see U.S. economic interests in the region counterbalancing militarization and promoting multilateralism.[114] Chinese scholars see opportunities for their country to work with the United States on Arctic issues, though some caution against "leaning to one side" due to the Sino-Russian partnership. An analysis of China's policy toward the U.S. chairmanship of the Arctic Council suggests bright prospects for

Sino-American cooperation in areas of priority to the United States, including climate change, improving living conditions in Arctic communities, and improving Arctic Ocean safety, security, and stewardship. The author, Ye Jiang, a senior research fellow at the Shanghai Institute for International Studies, highlights China's record of scientific research on climate change in the Arctic, as well as its participation in several Arctic Council working groups on environmental issues, and active role in the International Maritime Organization's efforts to develop a Polar Code to improve Arctic shipping safety.[115]

CHINA'S ARCTIC DIPLOMACY

Canada and Russia reportedly were the two countries most skeptical about China's entry into the Arctic Council as an observer, due their concern over Chinese recognition of their sovereignty claims over Arctic waters. A 2011 survey concluded that Canadians displayed the lowest level of support for including non-Arctic states in the Arctic Council.[116] Canadian scholars largely agree that China's interests and goals in the western Arctic focus on shipping, research, and resource development, though they differ in their assessments of China's broader intentions in the Arctic. Some analysts, such as Frédéric Lasserre of the University of Laval in Québec, view China's aims within the context of rising global interest in new shipping routes and see China's prospective role in the region as potentially advantageous for Canada in terms of cooperation in natural resource development, scientific collaboration, or tourism.[117] Other scholars, such as David Wright and Rob Huebert, both from the University of Calgary, are suspicious about China's broader geopolitical aims in the Arctic, including access to resources and diluting Canadian sovereignty.[118] P. Whitney Lackenbauer and James Manicom refute these interpretations, arguing that there are no grounds for asserting that China would reject Canadian sovereignty over the Northwest Passage.[119]

On April 5, 2016, the Chinese Maritime Safety Administration, subordinate to China's Transport Ministry, released a 365-page guidance on navigation in the Northwest Passage in an effort to promote the route as weather conditions enable its greater use for trade.[120] A 2014 voyage of the Canadian ore-carrier, *Nunavik*, from Quebec to Northeastern China, traveled 40 percent faster via the Northwest Passage than through the Panama Canal route. However, weather conditions still remain too uncertain for container shipping to be profitable along this route, which is more challenging for navigation than the NSR. Moreover, Chinese observers note that, for now, multiple permissions from Canadian governmental authorities complicate commercial use of the Northwest Passage, compared to Russia's more streamlined process with the NSR Administration. Canada also lacks Russia's large icebreaker fleet, and Canada's transportation infrastructure is relatively undeveloped in the Northwest Passage area, raising the risks in case of an accident or spill.[121]

As the Northwest Passage becomes navigable, the key question is whether or not the Chinese government will acknowledge Canadian sovereignty and request permission before sailing on what Canada considers to be its internal sea. The United States considers the waterway to be an international strait that accords all ships transit passage.[122] At an April 20, 2016 press conference, Foreign Ministry Spokesperson Hua Chunying sidestepped the issue:

> China noted that Canada considers this route as internal waters, while some countries believe it was open for international navigation. We also noted that Canada has imposed some restrictions on the use of the Northwest Passage, asking foreign vessels to inform the Canadian side and get permission before entering or crossing its exclusive economic zone and territorial waters. The Chinese side will make appropriate decisions by taking into account various factors.[123]

China's position on Canadian sovereignty over Arctic waters potentially affects U.S. interests in the region. The issue of sovereignty over the Northwest Passage as well as the Beaufort Sea has also complicated U.S.-Canadian relations, though the visit of newly elected Canadian Prime Minister Justin Trudeau to Washington in March 2016 appeared to usher in a new era of cooperation. The United States and Canada called for an international agreement to regulate fishing in the increasingly ice-free open Arctic, beyond the established economic zones of Arctic coastal states.[124]

Although, like Canada, Russia claims sovereignty over the NSR, the Arctic waters above its territory, Sino-Russian cooperation in the Arctic has been deepening of late. In November 2015, the Chinese Foreign Ministry spokesperson, Hong Lei, defined China's interests in the Arctic as they affect Sino-Russian relations as follows:

> China is an important stakeholder in the Arctic. China's participation in Arctic affairs has always been guided by three major principles: respect, cooperation and win-win results. We would like to enhance our communication and cooperation with all stakeholders

in Arctic affairs to jointly promote peace, stability and sustainable development of the Arctic region. Russia is a major country in the Arctic area and has significant influence on Arctic affairs. China-Russia Arctic cooperation enjoys sound basis. We stand ready to strengthen our exchanges and cooperation on Arctic affairs with the Russian side.[125]

As successive rounds of Western economic sanctions against Russia have an impact on the Russian energy industry, Russia is increasingly relying on China financially to develop energy resources in the Arctic. A $12 billion loan from China in April 2016 enabled Russia to move forward with its Yamal LNG project, for example, despite Western sanctions.[126] At the same time, China is wary of efforts by Russia to claim sovereignty to the Lomonosov Ridge, dividing the Eurasian and the Amerasian basins of the Arctic Ocean, which would limit Chinese access to the region.

For Russia, the development of the Arctic is a strategic priority. According to Russian President Vladimir Putin, the Arctic is "a concentration of practically all aspects of national security — military, political, economic, technological, environmental and that of resources."[127] Russia first issued a comprehensive Arctic strategy in 2008, *The Foundations of the Russian Federation's State Policy in the Arctic Until 2020 and Beyond*, and then in 2013 outlined, *Russian Strategy of the Development of the Arctic Zone and the Provision of National Security until 2020*.[128] According to these documents, Russia's objectives in the Arctic are:

- Development of the Arctic zone as a strategic resource base;
- Economic development to resolve socioeconomic development problems; and,

- Development of the NSR for shipping and transportation.

As melting ice in the Arctic facilitates energy exploration, China finds itself at a disadvantage, since these energy resources are largely located on the territory of Arctic states. Moreover, China lacks the cold water expertise necessary for exploration and has done little research, compared to Western oil majors, on the geology of Arctic energy resources.[129] Nonetheless, the Arctic is important to Chinese strategic calculations of its long-term energy security. A 2014 report by a research institute affiliated with the Chinese PLA portrayed the Arctic as a potential "lifeline" for the growing Chinese economy and urged greater energy cooperation with Arctic countries.[130]

Consequently, China has viewed resource cooperation with Russia in the Arctic with great interest. As Sino-Russian energy deals progressed in 2013, Chinese and Russian companies moved forward on a series of ventures in the Arctic, including exploring joint development projects between Rosneft and China National Petroleum Corporation (CNPC) in the Barents and Pechora Seas, as well as a LNG deal between the private gas company Novatek and CNPC for 3 million tons annually in gas deliveries from Yamal over a 15-year period.[131] Novatek ultimately agreed to sell CNPC a 20 percent stake in the Yamal LNG project and the deal was signed during Putin's May 2014 visit to China. According to the deal, CNPC would bring in 30 percent of the investment funds needed for the project and bring in other investors.[132] In 2014, CNPC purchased a 10 percent share in the Vankor oil and gas projects, the largest field discovered in the past 25 years. The Indian company, Oil and Natural Gas

Corporation Limited (ONGC), purchased a 15 percent stake in September 2015, and CNPC was reportedly considering additional investments. Also in September 2015, China Oil Services Limited, a subsidiary of China National Offshore Oil Company (CNOOC), agreed to drill two wells in the Sea of Okhotsk for a joint venture between Rosneft and Norway's Statoil.

As Alexander Gabuev noted, since the imposition of sanctions on Russia as a result of the conflict in Ukraine, Russian officials have become more receptive to Chinese investments in strategic sectors, such as oil and gas, as well as in infrastructure.[133] Moreover, the U.S. rebalancing to Asia, which China sees as seeking to constrain its rise, and tensions with the United States and other countries in the South China Sea, have contributed to greater overall Chinese interest in cooperating with Russia, including in the Arctic.[134]

Nonetheless, many domestic and international factors will affect progress in Sino-Russian Arctic energy deals, including international sanctions against Russia as a result of its actions in Ukraine, the low oil price, and China's economic downturn and the ongoing anti-corruption campaign, which has affected the ranks of CNPC. Thus the $20 billion loan that the CNPC — a state-owned firm that lost senior officials to Xi Jinping's anti-corruption campaign — initially pledged to Novatek (headed by a Gennadii Timchenko who is a close friend of Putin and now under Western sanctions) for the Yamal LNG project first shrank to $15 billion, then was never provided.[135] Instead, China's state-run Silk Road Fund purchased a 9.9 percent stake in the project.[136] Novatek ultimately secured the remaining $12 billion in needed external funding from the Export-Import Bank of China and China Development Bank, which typically are used for funding politically important projects and are less connected to global markets.[137] European banks are reluctant to fund Russian Arctic energy projects in light of the sanctions, making funding from China all the more important.[138]

After the first voyage by a Chinese commercial ship along the NSR in 2013, Yang Huigen, Director of China's Polar Shipping Institute, optimistically predicted that anywhere from 5-15 percent of China's trade could use the route by 2020.[139] Certainly, the prospects of greater shipping along this route have encouraged Sino-Russian cooperation in certain areas. Building on Sino-Russian energy cooperation, in 2010, Sovkomflot and CNPC signed an agreement on shipping oil along the NSR and providing training for the Chinese in arctic navigation.[140] Chinese companies are providing financing for infrastructure projects, for example, to facilitate coal shipments from Verkhoyansk Yakutiya to Shanghai.[141] The Chinese firm, Poly Technologies, is building a rail link from Archangelsk to the mining areas in the Urals and is interested in building a deepwater port in Archangelsk.[142]

There has also been some talk of involving the Russian Far East port of Zarubino in shipment of LNG from the Yamal fields, which would potentially facilitate Arctic LNG exports to the Asia-Pacific region, as well as to advance a long-sought goal by China's northeastern provinces to enhance infrastructure links between northern China and the Russian Far East. One Russian observer cautions, however, that this is a "phantom" project, in that budgetary woes have postponed indefinitely the implementation of a 2014 agreement by Russia's Summa Group with the Jilin province to build a deepwater port in Zarubino.[143]

Moreover, some Chinese claims about Arctic shipping are not supported by the facts. If, as stated earlier, one goal of the NSR is to improve energy security by overcoming their "Malacca dilemma" (that is, its fear of the U.S. closing of a key choke point of China's energy trade), the narrow passage through the Bering Straits is unlikely to improve the security picture much.[144] Turning to shipping itself, some Chinese scholars overstate the potential benefits of Arctic shipping and downplay its difficulties. For example, Guo Weiping of the Ocean University of China spoke of the northern shipping route as having the potential to "change the structure of global trade."[145]

Much like northeastern Chinese provinces seized on the Deng Xiaoping era concept of special economic zones to promote their regional interests, scholars from this part of China today view the Arctic route as a way of becoming involved in and benefiting from the One Belt One Road (OBOR) initiative. Thus, other scholars from the Dalian Ocean University in Liaoning province (in Northeastern China) argue that combining the new shipping possibilities in the Arctic with the OBOR initiative would have important consequences for the "greater Arctic."[146] Nonetheless, Chinese shipping companies have been as cautious as their Western counterparts have, and shipping along the NSR has thus far proceeded slowly. While exports of Arctic resources from Russia to China have been increasing gradually, Russian ships have largely been used to transport them. A recent survey of Chinese shipping companies showed that they were more interested in having access to the resources than in transiting shipments, due to the high risks and costs associated with Arctic shipping today.[147]

Although the impact of climate change in the Arctic on China is an important piece of the Chinese government's interest in the region, China is a relative newcomer to Arctic research. Thus far, China has been involved in seven scientific expeditions to the Arctic. Its seventh mission, now completed, had launched in July 2016, and involved French and American scientists.[148] In the future, China plans to cooperate with Russian scientists in a joint mission.[149] The two countries have yet to cooperate in Arctic research, though U.S. and Russian scholars have been cooperating in this area for many years and continue to do so despite political tensions.[150]

While cooperation has been proceeding between Russia and China in the Arctic, their interaction is complicated in this region by several factors. First, unlike any other sphere of their joint activity, this region is one where China finds itself in a relatively weak position compared to Russia. Russia has the advantage of being a coastal Arctic state with all of its attributes — territory, coastline, and indigenous people. China has none of these, not being physically located in or even near the Arctic. As one interesting analysis by Chinese scholars points out, this has an impact on the extent of Sino-Russian cooperation in the region. According to the authors, their cooperation is greatest in areas where China has the most to offer — in the area of resources — where China can be an investor and a buyer. The two countries also have shared interests in environmental protection and climate research, so there is the potential for cooperation there (though this has yet to happen). In other areas, such as shipping (where Russia is in a much stronger position), or military cooperation, the authors see limited prospects for cooperation.[151] Consequently, the authors conclude that China will only be able to achieve its goals in the Arctic with Russian cooperation, and that Russia's attitude toward Chinese participation will be important.[152] Others note that Russia's assistance will be needed for China to play the role it desires in the Arctic. Li and Zhang claim, for example, that the voyage of the Chinese icebreaker *Snow Dragon* in 2012 was only possible with Russian help because both Russia and the United States outpace China in technology, as well as in shipping data and navigation training, needed for the Arctic.[153] Moreover, until China has the icebreaker capability to operate independently of Russia in non-Russian areas of the Arctic, this will constrain China's ability to take advantage of any cost savings involved in Arctic passage and avoid Russian icebreaker escort fees.[154]

Although China succeeded in joining the Arctic Council in 2013, Russia initially was opposed. According to the U.S. diplomatic reporting released by WikiLeaks, Russia viewed the Arctic as its sphere of influence and favored an Arctic Council limited to Arctic states.[155] A number of reasons have been suggested for Russia's initial opposition to China's inclusion in the body: 1) the importance of the Arctic for Russian national security and the history of Arctic Russia as a zone closed to foreigners;[156] 2) lack of clarity about China's Arctic goals;[157] and, 3) reluctance to admit members with purely economic aims.[158] Both Canada and Russia, the countries with the longest Arctic borders, pressed for changes in the Arctic Council rules, requiring members to adhere to UNCLOS and the sovereign rights of Arctic states, as well as a new stipulation for a review of the status of observers every 4 years. When these were passed in 2011, this paved the way for the entry of China and several other non-Arctic states as observers in 2013.[159]

Prior to admission to the Arctic Council, some Chinese officials made statements that caused alarm in Russia. For example, in 2009, Deputy Foreign Minister Hu Zhengyue referred to the Arctic as the "common heritage of mankind."[160] In 2010, Admiral Yin Zhuo of the PLAN stated, "the Arctic does not belong to any particular nation and is rather the property of all the world's people" and argued that, based on its population, China should play an "indispensable role" in developing the region.[161] Since its admission as an observer to the Arctic Council, China has pledged to respect the sovereignty of Arctic states and follow UNCLOS with respect to Arctic seas, but Arctic states have the right to deny it some aspects of freedom of navigation on the grounds of reciprocity, as China does not recognize certain rights in its own coastal seas. The issues that may affect China's Arctic rights are its positions on foreign warships in its territorial sea, the routing of foreign cables, and foreign installations and structures on its continental shelf.[162]

Chinese scholars note the historical, geographic, and economic factors underlying Russian positions on Arctic sovereignty, which may serve to limit China's role.[163] Indeed, Russia has sought to demonstrate its sovereignty in a variety of ways, most dramatically in 2007 by planting a Russian flag on the Arctic shelf. At times Russia has proved willing to negotiate, as in 2010 when Russia and Norway ended their 40-year dispute over their boundary in the Barents Sea.[164] In February 2016, the Russian government submitted its claim to 1.2 million square kilometers of the Arctic seabed to the UN, including the shelf beneath the North Pole. This claim places Russia at odds with Canada over Arctic sovereignty.[165] Russia has been asserting this claim since 2002, but it was rejected previously for technical reasons.[166] All signatories to UNCLOS have the right to submit claims within 10 years of their ratification. The United States, which has not yet ratified the treaty, is thus unable to file any claims.

While shared norms about global politics bring Russia and China together on many global issues,[167] Russia's Arctic identity and China's emerging identity as a great power drive them apart on Arctic affairs. For Russia, the Arctic has assumed an important ideological importance in contemporary Russian nationalist narratives and related efforts to restore Russian greatness.[168] China, under Xi Jinping, has espoused an opportunistic worldview, and the Chinese President has urged his fellow citizens instead to showcase China's successes, take advantage of strategic opportunities, and strive for achievement (*fen fa you wei* 奋发有为).[169] This is a marked departure from the Deng Xiaoping era practice of keeping a low profile and downplaying capabilities to focus on domestic economic reform (*tao guang yang hui* 韬光养晦). Because of China's weaker position as an outsider in the Arctic, however, its opportunities lie in its interactions with smaller Arctic states, and opportunism is likely to be counterproductive in working cooperatively with Russia and other large Arctic states, Chinese scholars note.[170] Chinese leaders also play to a nationalistic audience at home, which is keen to relive China's age of exploration and is attentive to any slights by foreign countries. According to Polar scholar Anne-Marie Brady, "China talks down its interests in the Arctic to foreign audiences, meanwhile talking them up to domestic audiences."[171]

Other obstacles to Sino-Russian cooperation in the Arctic are more practical. The high-risk and high-cost energy projects face new challenges in light of Western sanctions on Russia (which limit Russia's access to needed technology, expertise, and investment), the low price of oil, and China's economic downturn and anti-corruption drive (which has hit CNPC, a partner in Russian Arctic projects).[172] Moreover, the practicality of Sino-Russian cooperation in these energy projects will also depend on the feasibility of transportation of the LNG from the Arctic to China.

While Canada and Russia have had some reservations about a greater Chinese role in the Arctic, Nordic countries have largely welcomed China's growing interest in the Arctic, as long as it adheres to UNCLOS on sovereignty and respects the rules and norms set by the Arctic Council. China invested considerable political capital in this effort, including visits by top leaders. In 2012, Hu Jintao made the first Chinese presidential visit to Denmark; and Wen Jiabao visited Sweden and Iceland, the first visit by a Chinese Prime Minister in several decades.[173] For the most part, Nordic states have understood Chinese motivations as commercial, though there were negative reactions to some Chinese investment plans in Iceland and Greenland.[174]

In the case of Iceland, fears turned out to be overblown. Although China signed its first free trade agreement (FTA) with the European state Iceland (which is not a part of the EU), and built a large new embassy in the capital, only five Chinese staff serve there, though some reports contend the mission could accommodate 100 times that number.[175] A bid by a Chinese investor, Huang Nubo, to purchase land in Iceland, allegedly for a golf course, was eventually rejected.[176] The disappearance in 2014 of China's Ambassador to Iceland, who was later accused of being a Japanese spy, further fueled suspicions about China.[177] Although certain sectors of Iceland's economy (e.g., geothermal energy and fishing) stand to gain from cooperation with China, public opinion on the new economic ties is decidedly mixed. A 2015 study showed lukewarm support for engagement with China, with 32 percent supporting, 34 percent opposed, and 34 percent neutral.[178] The study revealed the greatest support for collaborative scientific research, and the most concern over the reputational effects of cooperation with China due to its poor record on human rights, environmental protection, and labor issues, including the use of underpaid Chinese workers in previous projects to build two dams in Iceland.

Iceland, which faced a severe economic crisis in 2008, welcomed investment from China and saw an opportunity to develop economic relations with the country. This involved a $500 million currency swap deal in 2010, as well as investments in offshore energy. In return, Iceland became an enthusiastic supporter of China's entry into the Arctic Council, and now Iceland also hosts the Arctic Circle Assembly as a vehicle for open discussion of Arctic issues. For China, Iceland could become an important shipping hub and research base for its activities in the Arctic region.[179] China and Iceland are cooperating in building a joint facility to study the Northern Lights, funded by the Polar Research Institute of China, which has raised concern about China's potential use of the facility to track NATO flight movements. In 2014, Iceland's National Energy Authority granted a consortium including: the CNOOC, Iceland's Eyki Corporation, and Norway's Petoro, a license to explore for hydrocarbons on Iceland's northeast continental shelf.[180] China and Iceland also have developed substantial cooperation in geothermal energy and in mining for ferrosilicium, a key element of solar panels.[181]

China's ties with Greenland have also elicited concern, as the country seeks to develop its mining industry as a way of gaining further political autonomy from Denmark—Chinese investment may well be the vehicle for Greenland's independence. This would have important security consequences for U.S. basing rights and missile defense systems in the area.

In 2009, Greenland was granted self-rule from Denmark, which includes the right to develop its own resources as well as the right to independence.[182] For now, Greenland faces many economic and political challenges and remains a part of Denmark; therefore, it currently remains under NATO's umbrella.

After the Mineral Resources Act was passed in 2010, granting Greenland the rights to revenue earned through mining, the territory began reaching out to Chinese mining companies. Additional legislation, the Large Scale Project Act, gave Greenland the right to bring in foreign workers that led to concerns about the possibility of a major influx of Chinese workers in mining projects having a destabilizing effect on their environment under discussion.[183] Thus far, China has been involved in three mining projects in Greenland since 2009. Its first investment in the Arctic Circle involved Jiangxi Union, a consortium of companies (including Jiangxi Copper, one of the world's largest copper mining companies), in a venture prospecting for copper, zinc, and lead in eastern Greenland. Although this investment was significant, as it was China's first in the area, the low price of copper has limited its scope.[184]

The second investment, involving Chinese participation in a British iron-mining venture (London Mining), proved more controversial due to reports that it would employ 2,000 Chinese workers who would be exempt from Greenland's labor standards. This venture also exacerbated fears of China gaining control over the country's rich resource base.[185] London Mining eventually went bankrupt and a Hong Kong company, General Nice, that has ties to mining interests in central China, purchased its assets in January 2015. Although this is the first Arctic resource investment falling under Chinese control, the current low price of iron has made development of the Isua mine in Greenland unprofitable for now.[186]

The third investment, involving rare earths, has broader significance both within Greenland and geopolitically. China Nonferrous Metal Industry's Foreign Engineering and Construction Company, Limited (NFC), a Chinese state-owned company, first became involved in Greenland in 2011 in a joint venture to develop a zinc mine in the northeast of the territory. In 2014, the NFC signed a memorandum of understanding with a company in Greenland to develop rare earths and uranium mining in Kvanefjeld in southern Greenland.[187] Domestically, opponents of the project point to the environmental consequences, the tradeoff between development and seeking United Nations Educational, Scientific, and Cultural Organization (UNESCO) World Heritage Site status for the area to be mined (the site of a farming community since the days of the Vikings in the 10th century), and the impact on indigenous communities. There has also been opposition to the use of foreign workers, processing resources overseas, as well as to uranium mining more broadly (in 2013, legislation banning the extraction of radioactive materials was repealed). Geopolitically, the project has attracted controversy as developed countries seek to counter China's dominance over the rare earths market by acquiring alternative sources of supply. For Greenland, however, investment by non-EU companies, including Chinese firms, provides a boost for its efforts toward political autonomy from Denmark.

THE ARCTIC IN U.S.-CHINA RELATIONS

The Arctic is one of the few regions of the world where China finds itself at a disadvantage at present. Unlike the South China Sea or the Mekong River basin, where China is in a strong position relative to other states in the region and displays a preference for bilateral initiatives over multilateral ones, in the Arctic, the Chinese government takes the opposite tack, seeking to enhance multilateralism and displaying a preference for inclusive norms. For this reason, China sought to join the Arctic Council, the primary governance organization for the region, as an observer.

Twelve non-Arctic states now have observer status, including seven European countries (France, Germany, the Netherlands, Poland, Spain, the United Kingdom, and Italy), as well as five Asian states (China, Japan, Republic of Korea, Singapore, and India). Eleven intergovernmental and nine NGOs also have observer status.[188] Observers are included provisionally in the activities of the Arctic Council, "for such time as consensus exists among Ministers [of Arctic states]."[189] Observers participate in the activities of the Arctic Council's working groups, may submit related documents, and participate in particular projects along with Arctic states, as long as their financial contribution does not exceed that of Arctic states, unless the latter decide otherwise. The provisional status of Arctic observers stems from the authority of Arctic states to terminate the observer status of a state which "engages in activities that are at odds" with the Arctic Council's founding declaration or rules of procedure.[190]

China had applied for admission in 2007, some years before rapidly melting ice in the Arctic made greater participation in the economic development of the region by extra-regional actors a possibility. Discussion of its application was deferred until 2011, by which time a number of other countries had requested observer status, including the EU, India, Italy, Japan, South Korea, and Singapore, as well as a number of NGOs. The issue of admitting observers led to lengthy discussions among Arctic Council members, and no decision was reached until the May 2013 meeting.[191]

Despite restrictions on the participation of observer states, China's admission was particularly controversial and its interest in the Arctic Council has raised many questions for the international community, including the United States. One aspect of this was the possibility that large global players from outside the Arctic region would be able to dominate the Arctic Council.[192] Another concern is that the inclusion of outside great powers would lead to the militarization of the Arctic and bring their bilateral conflicts — Sino-Indian or Sino-Japanese tensions, for example — to the Arctic Council, thereby impeding regional consensus.[193] An April 2016 trilateral meeting on Arctic affairs, involving South Korea, Japan, and China, sought to reduce this prospect and enhance communication among the three Arctic Council observers.[194] The three countries also cooperate in the framework of the North Pacific Arctic Conference, an annual Track 2 undertaking that is co-sponsored by the East-West Center and the Korean Maritime Institute.[195]

Currently observers from outside the Arctic do in fact outnumber Arctic states, though their role is limited by the organization's rules, as noted above. Inflammatory statements by certain Chinese officials about their country's role in the Arctic, China's economic ties with Iceland (weakened by economic crisis), and resource deals by Chinese companies in the Arctic served to further suspicions about Chinese intentions in the Arctic Council and the region more broadly.

Canada and Russia, despite its strategic partnership with China, were the most resistant to granting China observer status. For Russia, it was imperative that all Arctic Council participants recognize Russian sovereignty in the Arctic, particularly its maritime sovereignty. Russia also sought to restrict decision-making to the five Arctic coastal states—the 2008 Russian Arctic policy document even omitted Arctic Council members Sweden, Finland, and Iceland from the group of states identified as having Arctic borders.[196] In a 2013 interview with Norwegian television, Prime Minister Dmitry Medvedev asserted that while it was reasonable that several countries outside the region joined the Arctic Council, and that Russia trusted China and wanted to cooperate with it, "the regulations operating in the Arctic Region should be governed by the Arctic States themselves."[197] This was less than a year before the Russian takeover of Crimea, however, and since the imposition of sanctions by the EU and the United States, which have complicated Russia's quest for investment in its Arctic regions, Russia has become much more open to economic participation by Asian states, including China, in the region. In August 2015, Foreign Minister Sergei Lavrov welcomed the participation of Arctic Council observer states in the economic projects approved by the forum, but referred to China as a "priority partner" for Arctic projects in resources, science, and technology. In Lavrov's view, China and Russia should collaborate bilaterally in the Arctic, not just within the scope of Arctic Council projects.[198]

While Russia reportedly was more concerned about the EU becoming an observer of the Arctic Council—that would greatly enhance European influence over the forum since EU states were already members and observers—Canada was more concerned about the impact of Asian observer states, particularly China.[199] For Canada, as for Russia, recognition of its sovereignty, particularly over the Northwest Passage, and respect for the rights of indigenous peoples are key priorities that the Canadian government wants to see observer states recognize. Moreover, given Canada's leading role in the creation of the Arctic Council, Canadians have been resistant to moves to "internationalize" the forum and dilute the jurisdiction and authority of Arctic states and peoples over their own affairs.[200]

While the Nordic Arctic Council member states share Russian and Canadian concerns about observer states recognizing their sovereignty and authority over Arctic matters, Nordic countries have been more welcoming of Asian observer states, including China. Unlike Canada and Russia, Nordic states recognize the global economic and commercial interests in the Arctic. With Asian shipping and resource companies already interested and investing in the region, Nordic Arctic Council members preferred to involve Asian states in the forum and ensure their commitment to Arctic norms rather than see these non-Arctic countries coalesce outside of the body in support of narrower interests.[201] China has sought to build on the warmer reception by the Nordic States to expand its soft power in the region and further legitimize its claim to be an Arctic stakeholder by proposing and developing the China-Nordic Arctic Research Center in Shanghai to further cooperation between scholars from China and Nordic Arctic states. The new center opened in December 2013 to support joint research on climate change, Arctic economic development, and shipping.[202]

The U.S. position was somewhere in-between Canadian and Russian wariness and Northern European inclusiveness. Before the 2013 meeting that decided on the inclusion of China and other Asian observers, an American official told the British Broadcasting Corporation (BBC) that the United States was open to observers and considered China to be a responsible applicant.[203] Moreover, China's observer status in the Arctic Council would provide Secretary of State John Kerry with an additional forum within which to engage China (as well as India) on climate change, a key priority for the Obama administration. Nonetheless, some U.S. officials admitted to sharing some of the concerns expressed by Canada and Russia, though they noted the difficulty of supporting the admission of allies like Japan and South Korea, but not China.[204]

According to Leiv Lunde, a Norwegian scholar and former official in the Norwegian Ministry of Foreign Affairs, the United States was undecided until the very last moment about granting observer status to China.[205] After a spirited dinner debate at the 2013 Arctic Council meeting in Kiruna, Sweden, Secretary of State Kerry reportedly brokered a compromise that paved the way for the admission of China and several other states as observers.[206] The compromise involved requiring observers to agree to specific rules for their conditional participation, particularly recognizing the sovereignty of Arctic states and UNCLOS as the determining legal framework.[207] According to the Arctic Council's manual *Arctic Council Rules of Procedure*, for observers to be admitted they must abide by what one expert has termed the "seven Arctic Council commandments:"[208]

1. Accepts and supports the objectives of the Arctic Council defined in the Ottawa declaration;
2. Recognizes Arctic States' sovereignty, sovereign rights and jurisdiction in the Arctic;
3. Recognizes that an extensive legal framework applies to the Arctic Ocean including, notably, the Law of the Sea, and that this framework provides a solid foundation for responsible management of this ocean;
4. Respects the values, interests, culture and traditions of Arctic indigenous peoples and other Arctic inhabitants;
5. Has demonstrated a political willingness as well as financial ability to contribute to the work of the Permanent Participants and other Arctic indigenous peoples;
6. Has demonstrated their Arctic interests and expertise relevant to the work of the Arctic Council; and,
7. Has demonstrated a concrete interest and ability to support the work of the Arctic Council, including through partnerships with member states and Permanent Participants bringing Arctic concerns to global decision-making bodies.[209]

Another analysis argues that there was no opposition within the United States or other Arctic states to China *per se* becoming an observer of the Arctic Council, but to having additional extra-regional observers in general, with bigger powers seeing the Arctic as a domestic issue, not a global one.[210] Privately, however, some U.S. officials convey some continued skepticism about China's long-term intentions in the Arctic — for example, its potential to exploit economic weakness in the Nordic states or to take advantage of opportunities to engage in scientific research to improve anti-submarine warfare capabilities — while others argue that it is preferable to include China in discussions of Arctic governance to encourage its compliance.[211]

During former President Obama's visit to Alaska in early September 2015, the PLAN sent five warships into U.S. territorial waters in the Bering Sea (within 12 miles of the Aleutian Islands) to exercise their right of innocent passage according to UNCLOS.[212] This means that the ships have the right to traverse the area as long as they do not engage in any activities that may cause a threat to security, such as military exercises or intelligence gathering, or take any other actions (fishing, research, etc.) beyond sailing through the area. The ships (three surface combatants, an amphibious warship, and an oiler) were part of a group of seven that had participated in a joint naval exercise with Russia in August. Although it was an unusual coincidence that the Chinese ships appeared in the Bering Strait for the first time during Obama's visit to the area, the passage of the PLAN ships more likely was timed to coincide with Chinese celebrations of the 70th anniversary of World War II—China's military parade began just hours after the ships were sighted in U.S. waters—and the lead up to President Xi Jinping's visit to the United States later in September 2015.[213]

The U.S. Chairmanship of the Arctic Council provides additional opportunities to engage China on areas of common concern, such as climate change. In the short term, the international community has struggled to move forward with agreements to address climate change that are palatable to developed and developing countries alike. A Chinese delegation attended the GLACIER conference, but China (as well as India and Russia) refused to sign the non-binding declaration calling for more effort to address climate change, raising questions about China's position on the balance of interests between protecting the Arctic environment, and developing its resources.[214] According to one Chinese media report, the Chinese government needed more time to study the document in preparation for the November 2015 Paris climate talks, though a Russian analysis suggested that China, India, and Russia shared concerns about the economic costs of measures to address climate change.[215]

In October 2015, the Arctic States agreed to develop cooperation in the Arctic among their Coast Guard agencies with the creation of the Arctic Coast Guard Forum.[216] As a non-Arctic state, China is not a member of this group, but the United States cooperates with the Chinese Coast Guard through the North Pacific Coast Guard Forum, which also includes Canada, Japan, Russia, and the Republic of Korea. The North Pacific Coast Guard Forum, which served as a model for the Arctic Coast Guard Forum, holds bilateral and multilateral exercises to improve maritime safety and security and develop procedures for various contingencies. Additionally, the U.S. and Chinese Coast Guards reportedly are finalizing the details of an agreement to improve their communication. The agreement under discussion would be similar to the 2014 multilateral Code for Unplanned Encounters at Sea the two countries have signed, which seeks to avoid miscommunication among navies.

Since 1993, the United States and China have been cooperating in patrolling the northern Pacific Ocean for high seas driftnet fishing in an effort to implement UN General Assembly Resolution 46/215 that prohibits the practice. The U.S.-China memorandum on cooperation in this area is known as the U.S.-China Shiprider Agreement because it outlines procedures for Chinese officials to board U.S. Coast Guard vessels to improve communication and enforcement of the prohibition against driftnet fishing. This agreement also allows law enforcement officials of either country to board and inspect a U.S. or Chinese flagged ship suspected of driftnet fishing.[217] For example, the U.S. and Chinese Coast Guards cooperated in June 2014 in apprehending a Chinese vessel, the *Yi Yuan*, that was engaged in large-scale illegal driftnet fishing.[218]

In November 2015, U.S. Special Representative for the Arctic Admiral Papp testified to the House of Representatives on U.S. Arctic priorities. Among them was the effort to prevent unregulated fishing in international waters in the Central Arctic Ocean. Currently, there is no commercial fishing in this area, but climate change may alter the situation in the future. The United States passed a law in 2009 banning fishing in its own exclusive economic zone (EEZ) north of the Bering Strait until there was sufficient information about fish stocks in the area. Canada also passed a similar law in 2014. Both were responding to the collapse of stocks of pollock in the 1980s as a result of overfishing in an area of the Bering Strait known as the Donut Hole. An international agreement eventually was signed in 1994, but this was too late for the already depleted pollock.[219] In July 2015, the five Arctic coastal states plus China, Japan, and South Korea signed an unbinding declaration on unregulated fishing.[220] Negotiations toward an enhanced governance mechanism—by either creating a binding agreement (the option proposed by the United States), a monitoring organization, or a broader non-binding agreement—have proceeded regularly, thus far meeting in December 2015 and April 2016. While some U.S. officials were heartened by China's interest in participating in a precautionary voluntary regulatory framework, a Greenpeace activist cautioned that the measures proposed thus far are inadequate and may be a cover for the interests of countries in exploiting fisheries in the Arctic when this becomes feasible in the future.[221]

There have been some limited exchanges of views between the United States and China on polar issues since 2011 within the framework of the Strategic and Economic Dialogue, as well as a series of workshops on U.S.-China Arctic Policy, involving academic and government experts, first in Shanghai in May 2015, and then in Washington, DC, in May 2016.[222] Nonetheless, the Arctic has not yet played a major role in U.S.-China diplomacy, which may reflect the relative lack of importance of the Arctic on their bilateral agenda, compared to hot button issues such as the South China Sea, trade, and human rights, or the relatively modest role the Arctic has played in U.S. foreign policy to date.

Interestingly, the Arctic is one area where the United States and China agree on the need for freedom of navigation, though China has yet to directly state its position on Canadian sovereignty over the Northwest Passage or Russian sovereignty claims on the Lomonosov ridge. The Chinese government finds itself in a bind here—siding with the United States on freedom of the seas in the Arctic, while beneficial for Chinese economic interests in the region, would nonetheless open China to criticism of its more restrictive definitions of sovereignty on "near seas" such as the South China Sea and also adversely affect Sino-Russian relations.[223]

For all its ambiguity, China's Arctic policy has attracted considerable scrutiny, to the point of inquiring if China feigns to observe global or regional norms only to subvert them, and uses international law as a weapon, an approach known as lawfare. According to this viewpoint, the Chinese government uses the law (in this case the UNCLOS) to constrain its opponent and exert psychological pressure by framing the media debate and influencing global public opinion, for example, by asserting that the Arctic is a global commons.[224] One widely cited analysis (though the author was an undergraduate student at the time) suggested that China used lawfare "to circumvent its weaker status as a non-Arctic state through asymmetrical means."[225] Most scholars fail to see any evidence of China actively seeking to undermine Arctic norms or misuse UNCLOS, though they point to efforts to take advantage of ambiguities within it and to advance Chinese interests in the region incrementally.[226]

CONCLUSION

China is playing a long game in the Arctic. The Arctic is the one area of the world where it remains at a disadvantage, despite its emergence as a global power and its economic and scientific interests in the region. China fears being excluded from future economic and scientific opportunities because of its current modest voice on Arctic affairs. In the short term, China is limited by its observer status on the Arctic Council and its technological/military capability. Within the existing governance framework, China will continue to advocate that the forum take into account the legitimate interests of non-Arctic states and the common interests of the international community.[227] Because of the restrictions on China's role in the Arctic Council, the primary institution for Arctic governance, in the long term, China may try to seek changes in existing governance to better accommodate its interests. The trilateral meeting of Chinese, Japanese, and South Korea

Foreign Ministers—all three Arctic Council observer states—to discuss Arctic issues may be a step in this direction.

Many Western experts see China pursuing an Arctic policy that supports its grand strategy to shape the international order in such a way that China's interests as a global power are accommodated. This involves expanding Chinese military and economic capabilities, advancing Chinese interests incrementally and defending Chinese sovereignty, while avoiding confrontation.[228] The commitment of the Chinese government to expanding its icebreaker capability, China's Arctic diplomacy, and the involvement of Chinese companies in resource deals in the region are also steps in this direction, but the road ahead is far from clear. Since China has yet to release an Arctic strategy, it is premature to link it to China's grand strategy. Moreover, although President Xi Jinping has concentrated more foreign policymaking authority in his own hands than many of his predecessors, multiple Chinese interests are involved in China's Arctic policy, with potentially different agendas. These include the PLAN, the Foreign Ministry, the State Oceanic Administration, the Chinese shipping and resource extracting companies, just to name a few.[229] As with the South China Sea,[230] multiple participants in the policy process about the Arctic may lead to contradictory policies that result in increasing tensions in the region. Thus far, the lack of clarity about China's intentions in the Arctic has increased suspicion, even with close partners such as Russia.

Some of China's interests in the Arctic overlap with its Asian security agenda, including its aim to improve its energy security by diversifying its sources of supply and supply routes.[231] Access to Russia's Arctic resources, in the long term, would help China overcome its "Malacca dilemma," that is its fear that opponents or hostile forces could block its access to needed energy supplies through the narrow choke point. We also see Chinese companies and the Chinese government pursuing in the Arctic the aims of infrastructure development and resource extraction that are central to China's One Belt One Road initiative for Central Asia, South Asia, and Southern Europe. Not surprisingly, China's northeastern provinces, which have struggled to find sufficient employment opportunities for workers in the shrinking state-owned enterprise sector, are eager to encourage a "new Silk Road" to the Arctic to lift up their own economic fortunes.

Nonetheless, the U.S. is an Arctic coastal state and necessarily has more diverse, strategic, and domestic interests at play in the Arctic than does China. Since the end of the Cold War, the United States has sought to redefine its interests in the Arctic, and China's growing interest in the region comes at a time of flux in the U.S. understanding of its own role there. Economic opportunities, the impact of climate change, and shifts in great power relations all have served to motivate a greater commitment of U.S. resources to develop infrastructure and icebreaker capabilities, and maintain, if not expand, military forces in the region.

China's actions in the Arctic in the short term have the greatest impact on U.S. global priorities, including the economic and political stability of Europe, freedom of navigation, and strategic concerns in other areas, such as the role of Russia in Europe and of China in the South China Sea. In the Nordic countries, China has been acting like a savvy realtor eying a remote exurb for future growth potential—China has engaged the most economically vulnerable areas, such as Iceland

and Greenland, earning goodwill and a foothold from which to take advantage of unfolding opportunities. Both Iceland and Greenland have their own domestic political and economic concerns—Iceland being outside the EU and recovering from the 2008 economic crisis, and Greenland seeking greater autonomy from Denmark—that create a favorable climate for Chinese overtures; at the same time, their security value to the United States has increased in light of current tensions with Russia in Northern Europe in the wake of the Ukraine conflict.

In addition to their consequences for U.S. Security interests in Northern Europe, China's actions in the Arctic also affect the U.S. priority on freedom of navigation. The transit of Chinese naval vessels in the U.S. EEZ in the Bering Strait in September 2015 appeared to some U.S. observers to indicate acceptance by China of the principle of freedom of navigation, which Chinese officials have rejected in reference to the passage of U.S. Navy ships in areas China claims to be in their territorial waters in the South China Sea.[232] In a May 2016 press conference, however, Foreign Ministry Spokesman Lu Kang argued that freedom of navigation for commercial versus military vessels were "completely different things," and that UNCLOS does not specifically allow innocent passage for military ships that he described as "[willfully] trespassing."[233]

Although China is concerned about Canadian and Russian sovereignty claims potentially limiting Chinese shipping opportunities or at least raising their cost due to tariffs, the Chinese government has not specifically commented on their claims. Considering China's investment in political capital, military assets, and infrastructure in defending its sovereignty in East Asia, China may well take advantage of freedom of navigation when it is possible, as with the U.S. EEZ in the Bering Strait, but tacitly at least support Canadian and Russian sovereignty over what they view as their internal waters to enlist their support for China's claims in East Asia.[234]

Russia is the gatekeeper for China's access to the NSR. Although Russia had reservations about China's acceptance as an Arctic Council observer (like Canada, and the United States to a lesser extent), since the conflict in Ukraine and its resulting sanctions, Russian officials have welcomed China's investment in the Russian Arctic. Many analysts overestimate the current differences between Russia and China in the Arctic and undervalue the Sino-Russian partnership as a whole.[235] At least while Putin and Xi Jinping remain in presidential office in their respective countries, Sino-Russian relations in the Arctic are likely to remain cooperative, as Russia needs Chinese investments in energy and infrastructure in the Russian Arctic, and China needs Russian escorts, training in Arctic navigation, and opportunities for economic involvement in the region.

Prior to 2014, Russia vacillated between its desire for control over a strategically important region and its increasing need for partners to develop its resources. The latter has worked to China's advantage since then and enabled more Sino-Russian cooperation in the Arctic than might have been predicted a few years ago. Nationalism in both countries undermines this trend, however, by urging greater control for Russia and leading to assertions in China of its perceived rights in the Arctic, which could lead to Sino-Russian tensions in the region in the future.[236]

Future developments in the Arctic have the potential to reshape Sino-Russian relations overall very fundamentally, however — a prospect that neither country is prepared to address.

As the international community seeks to maintain the pace of climate change within manageable
parameters — optimistically a 2 degree Celsius or 3.6
degree Fahrenheit change — scenarios for more severe
or even catastrophic changes bode ill for Sino-Russian
relations in the Arctic and in general.[237] China's rural
population will disproportionately bear the burden
of climate change effects, which, in China's northern
breadbasket, will involve further water scarcity, de-
sertification, and threats to food security.[238] For example, China's 2016 Climate Assessment Report states:

> shrinking of river flows caused by the melting away of
> glaciers in western China may lead to struggles over
> cross-border water resources and surges of transna-
> tional migration, triggering international disputes and
> conflict.[239]

In the long term, such pressures may lead to internal
migration and as well to pressures in the Sino-Russian
border regions over access to water, land, and food,
which could in turn result in environmental migration
of Chinese citizens to Russia.

The Arctic itself is both a contributor to climate
change and its victim, creating a particular burden for
Arctic states and non-Arctic stakeholders, who thus
far have focused more on short-term and mid-term
issues, such as boundary demarcation and resource
exploration, than on the region's future. Although
climate change has enabled economic cooperation to
develop in the Arctic, the use of obtained fossil fuel resources then contribute to adverse trends in the region,
such as sea water rises and changes in weather pat-
terns, with negative consequences for other countries
outside the region as well as the Arctic itself. What is
needed, Oran Young argues, is a new and more com-

prehensive approach to Arctic governance that can better anticipate and address long-term challenges.[240] For this to occur, however, major stakeholders have to agree on the nature of these challenges and the steps needed to address them. Given China's need for resources to maintain its economic growth trajectory, the most elusive form of Sino-American cooperation in the Arctic may yet be over the urgency of addressing climate change.

POLICY IMPLICATIONS

Implication 1.

Although it may be useful to raise the inconsistencies between China's views on sovereignty and freedom of navigation in the Arctic and the South China Sea, linkage between the two is unlikely to work. Under Xi Jinping's leadership, the Chinese government has become increasingly entrenched in its assertion of its sovereign rights in East Asia, and these aims are unlikely to be moderated for access to future opportunities in the Arctic. China's Arctic aims support the country's overall interest in taking advantage of opportunities befitting a global power, but the Chinese government's defense of its sovereignty in East Asia relates to core interests that are viewed as central to the country's political stability and identity.

Implication 2.

China and the United States have many common interests in the Arctic, including maritime safety, addressing unregulated driftnet fishing, and avoiding oil spills. Moreover, U.S. and Chinese Coast Guards have cooperated for many years and developed relationships that are useful to address future contingencies in the Arctic and elsewhere in the world. The United States and China should continue to develop operational level relationships to address their common concerns in the Arctic.

Implication 3.

The United States should engage its Asian allies, Japan and South Korea, as well as its Asian partners like Singapore and India on Arctic issues. It is not in the U.S. interest or in that of the Arctic Council for observer states to coalesce outside the forum and, during its last year as Chairman, the United States should develop a better outreach strategy to all Asian states with interests in the Arctic. This could focus on shared interests such as shipping, fishing, or minerals exploration, or concerns such as climate change, maritime safety, and Arctic navigation.

Implication 4.

China faces reputational barriers in northern Europe, who traditionally has been concerned with human rights, to expanding its influence in the Arctic. China's resource investments in Africa, South America, and Asia have revealed its disregard for environmental and human rights issues in its areas of investment. Nonetheless, China's resource investments in the Arctic may enable China to further institutionalize its presence there in the future, as China did with its naval base in Djibouti, Africa, which followed a pattern of Chinese resource investments in Africa.

Implication 5.

There is no "Great Game" in the Arctic. For the most part, since the end of the Cold War, cooperation has characterized the region. In recent years, however, issues from outside the Arctic have cast a shadow on it, including the European financial crisis and the tensions between NATO and Russia. China has taken advantage of these problems to expand its own influence in the Arctic by improving its ties with both Iceland and Russia.

Implication 6.

The United States needs to distinguish between U.S.-Russia tensions in Europe and our relations in the Arctic and keep Russian Arctic actions in perspective. Russia has the longest coastline in the Arctic Circle and needs to invest in infrastructure to develop it. Discussion of an "icebreaker gap" is not very helpful—it would make no sense for the United States to compete with Russia, which has an extensive Arctic coastline, in the deployment of icebreakers, nor do we have the resources or rationale to do so.

Implication 7.

Although the Arctic has been relatively insulated from interstate conflicts since the end of the Cold War, the region now risks becoming involved in a security dilemma dynamic, according to which uncertainties about Russian intentions drive NATO to take counteractions which then lead to a Russian response, and so forth.[241] The necessity of sanctions against Russia notwithstanding, some confidence building measures would be useful in the Arctic to restore trust among the regional states and reduce the likelihood of militarizing the region in response to developments outside it.

Implication 8.

There is at times a mismatch between available governance mechanisms in the Arctic and the issues at stake, as the Arctic Council is restricted from addressing security issues. The need for a mechanism to address operational security issues, such as maritime safety, led, for example, to the creation of the Arctic Coast Guard forum. However, after the Russian takeover of Crimea, Russian experts were not included in 2014 experts meetings about the new organization, and sanctions against Russia over Ukraine have reduced Russian involvement in other fora dealing with Arctic issues. This is shortsighted as it would be difficult to address most Arctic issues (maritime safety and oil spills, for example) without Russian participation.

Implication 9.

Experts have suggested a variety of mechanisms to address security issues:
- Make use of existing security fora such as the Nordic Defense Ministers, the Arctic Security Conference, and include Russian participation. Since Russia is a primary security concern for Nordic states, excluding Russia from these venues is counter-productive.
- Reform the Arctic Council along the lines of the Organization of Security and Cooperation in Europe to include a "basket" or component for

addressing security issues, in addition to maintaining the focus on indigenous communities, and economic and environmental issues that the current Arctic Council has.[242]

- Hold a meeting of heads of states of Arctic states to address security concerns that threaten to militarize the region and shift it away from its environmental and economic priorities.[243]

Although European regional cooperation mechanisms have inspired much of the discussion about Arctic governance, Asia's experience is also relevant. For example, a regular forum for high-level political dialogue on Arctic issues could be patterned on the East Asian Summit mechanism for East Asia. To include security issues in the discussion and develop confidence-building measures, a broader forum could be created similar to the Association of Southeast Asian Nations (ASEAN) Regional Forum that brings together outsiders and insiders to address common security issues.

Implication 10.

The United States also needs to pursue a long game in the Arctic, involving long-term investments in infrastructure such as icebreakers and deepwater ports, as well as personnel, such as the Army's 4th Brigade Combat Team, and a commitment to the scientific understanding of climate change in the region. Because of the long lead times in developing infrastructure, especially icebreakers, decisions cannot be contingent on short-term commercial prospects, and need to take into account future contingencies in terms of the growing accessibility of the Arctic to a wider range of actors with goals and practices that potentially differ from those of the United States. Access to the Arctic will only grow, leaving the United States open to new threats as well as opportunities.

Implication 11.

It is difficult for the United States to assert its interests in the Arctic or protest their infringement without ratifying UNCLOS. As the only Arctic state that has not ratified the agreement, we are marginalized on important discussions of its application, including with China. The current administration should make this a priority.

ENDNOTES

1. Kenneth J. Bird, Ronald R. Charpentier, Donald L. Gautier, David W. Houseknecht, Timothy R. Klett, Janet K. Pitman, Thomas E. Moore, Christopher J. Schenk, Marilyn E. Tennyson, and Craig J. Wandrey, "Circum-Arctic Resource Appraisal: Estimates of Undiscovered Oil and Gas North of the Arctic Circle," USGS Fact Sheet 2008-3049, Washington, DC: U.S. Geological Survey, p. 1, available from *https://pubs.usgs.gov/fs/2008/3049/fs2008-3049.pdf*.

2. Philip Budzik, "Arctic Oil and Natural Gas Potential," Washington, DC: U.S. Energy Information Administration, Office of Integrated Analysis and Forecasting, Oil and Gas Division, October 2009, p. 6, available from *www.eia.gov/oiaf/analysispaper/arctic/pdf/arctic_oil.pdf*.

3. U.S. Environmental Protection Agency, "Climate Change Indicators in the United States: Arctic Sea Ice," Washington, DC: U.S. Environmental Protection Agency, June 2015, p. 3, available from *https://www3.epa.gov/climatechange/pdfs/print_sea-ice-2015.pdf*.

4. Picture sourced from *Ibid.*, p. 2.

5. Figure sourced from NASA Earth Observatory, Image of the Day, "Arctic Sea Ice Drops below 2007 Record," August 26, 2012, available from *earthobservatory.nasa.gov/IOTD/view.php?id=78994*.

6. National Snow and Ice Data Center, "Sea Ice Hits Record Lows," December 6, 2016, available from *nsidc.org/arcticseaice-news/*.

7. Chart sourced from *Ibid*.

8. "Mission Accomplished: Crystal Serenity Completes 32-day Northwest Passage Journey," Press Archive, Los Angeles, CA: Crystal Cruises, September 16, 2016, available from *legacy.crystalcruises.com/MediaCenter.aspx*; Karen Schwartz, "As Global Warming Thaws Northwest Passage, a Cruise Sees Opportunity," *The New York Times*, July 6, 2016, available from *www.nytimes.com/2016/07/10/travel/arctic-cruise-northwest-passage-greenpeace.html*.

9. Headquarters, U.S. Coast Guard, *Arctic Strategy*, Washington, DC: U.S. Coast Guard, May 2013, p. 13, available from *https://www.uscg.mil/seniorleadership/DOCS/CG_Arctic_Strategy.pdf*; Glenn M. Sulmasy and Andrew P. Wood, *U.S. Coast Guard Activity in the Arctic Region*, Law of the Sea Occasional Paper, No. 6, University of California, Berkeley, Institute for Legal Research, 2014, pp. 9-10; U.S. Government Accountability Office, *Maritime Infrastructure: Key Issues Related to Commercial Activity in the U.S. Arctic over the Next Decade: Report to Congressional Requesters*, GAO-14-299, Washington, DC: U.S. Government Accountability Office, March 2014, p. 23; Ronald O'Rourke, *Coast Guard Maritime Infrastructure: Key Issues Related to Commercial Activity in the U.S. Arctic over the Next Decade: Report to Congressional Requesters*, Washington, DC: U.S. Library of Congress, Congressional Research Service, May 27, 2016, pp. 2-5.

10. Table sourced from O'Rourke, *Coast Guard Polar Icebreaker Modernization*, p. 10, note was prepared by the Congressional Research Service based on a U.S. Coast Guard chart showing data compiled by the Coast Guard as of May 21, 2015.

11. Matt Miller, "Coast Guard Maps Out Marine Traffic Lanes to Arctic," Alaska Public Media, January 29, 2015, available from *www.alaskapublic.org/2015/01/29/coast-guard-maps-out-marine traffic-lanes-to-the-arctic/*.

12. Robert K. Headland, "Transits of the Northwest Passage to End of the 2014 Navigation Season," Scott Polar Research Institute, University of Cambridge, October 14, 2014, pp. 9-11; "Northern Sea Route Shipping Statistics," PAME: Protection of the Artic Marine Environment, n.d., available from *www.pame.is/index.php/ projects/arctic-marine-shipping/northern-sea-route-shipping-statistics*.

13. Figure reprinted from Chief of Naval Operations, *The United States Navy Arctic Roadmap for 2014 to 2030,* Washington, DC: U.S. Department of the Navy, February 2014, p. 11, available from *www.navy.mil/docs/USN_arctic_roadmap.pdf*.

14. *Ibid.*, pp. 11-13.

15. Figure reprinted from *Ibid.,* p. 14.

16. Kevin Schaefer, "All about Frozen Ground: Methane and Frozen Ground," National Snow & Ice Data Center, available from *https://nsidc.org/cryosphere/frozenground/methane.html*.

17. Lamont-Doherty Earth Observatory, Columbia University, "Greenland's 2015 melt records consistent with 'Arctic amplification'," Science Daily, June 9, 2016, available from *https://www. sciencedaily.com/releases/2016/06/160609064532.htm*.

18. Terry Fenge, "The Arctic Council: Past, Present, and Future Prospects with Canada in the Chair from 2013 to 2015," *The Northern Review*, Vol. 37, Fall 2013, pp. 10-12.

19. "National Security Decision Memorandum 144," Washington, DC: U.S. National Security Council, December 22, 1971, available from *fas.org/irp/offdocs/nsdm-nixon/nsdm-144.pdf*.

20. National Security Council, National Security Decision Directive (NSDD) Number 90, Washington, DC: The White House, April 14, 1983, available from *https://reaganlibrary.archives.gov archives/reference/NSDDs.html#.WFf-wke7ppg*.

21. National Security Presidential Directive 66, Homeland Security Presidential Directive 25, "Arctic Region Policy," Washington, DC: The White House, January 9, 2009, pp. 2-3, available from *https://www.hsdl.org/?collection&id=2481&pid=gwb*.

22. *Ibid.*, pp. 3-4.

23. *Ibid.*, p. 4.

24. Barack Obama, *National Security Strategy*, Washington, DC: The White House, May 2010, p. 50.

25. Ronald O'Rourke, *Changes in the Arctic: Background and Issues for Congress*, Washington, DC: U.S. Library of Congress, Congressional Research Service, December 21, 2015, p. 64, available from *https://www.hsdl.org/?abstract&did=789281*.

26. Barack Obama, *National Strategy for the Arctic Region*, Washington, DC: The White House, May 2013, available from *https://obamawhitehouse.archives.gov/sites/default/files/docs/nat_arctic_strategy.pdf*.

27. Headquarters, U.S. Coast Guard, *Arctic Strategy*, p. 22.

28. *Ibid.*, pp. 23-26.

29. U.S. Department of Defense (DoD), *Arctic Strategy*, Washington, DC: U.S. Department of Defense, November 2013, p. 4, available from *archive.defense.gov/pubs/2013_Arctic_Strategy.pdf*.

30. *Implementation Plan for the National Strategy for the Arctic Region*, Washington, DC: The White House, January 2014, pp. 5-11, available from *https://obamawhitehouse.archives.gov/sites/default/files/docs/implementation_plan_for_the_national_strategy_for_the_arctic_region_-_fi....pdf*.

31. O'Rourke, *Changes in the Arctic*, p. 57.

32. Chief of Naval Operations, *The United States Navy Arctic Roadmap for 2014 to 2030*, p. 15.

33. *Ibid.*, p. 17.

34. The United States was Chairman in 1998-2000 and will occupy the role again in 2031-33. See O'Rourke, *Changes in the Arctic*, p. 11.

35. Quote from U.S. Secretary of State John Kerry, Chair of the Arctic Council, see Arctic Council Official website, "About U.S. Chairmanship," available from *www.arctic-council.org/index.php/ en/about-us/arctic-council/u-s-chairmanship.*

36. Arctic Council Official website, "Frequently Asked Questions," November 4, 2016, available from *www.arctic-council.org/ index.php/en/about-us/arctic-council/faq.*

37. "Declaration on the Establishment of the Arctic Council (Ottawa, Canada, 1996)," Global Affairs Canada, Government of Canada, available from *www.international.gc.ca/arctic-arctique/ ottdec-decott.aspx?lang=eng.*

38. Nils Wang, "Arctic Security — An Equation with Multiple Unknowns," *Journal of Military and Strategic Studies*, Vol. 15, No. 2, 2013, p. 17.

39. *Ibid.*, p. 23.

40. Heather Conley, "America's New Foreign Policy Frontier," *Polar Initiative Policy Brief Series Arctic 2014: Who Gets a Voice and Why it Matters*, Washington, DC: Wilson Center Polar Initiative, September 2014, p. 3. Her earlier report also criticized the management of Arctic policy in the U.S. government, see Heather A. Conley, Terry Toland, Mihaela David, and Natalja Jegorova, *The New Foreign Policy Frontier: U.S. Interests and Actors in the Arctic*, Washington, DC: Center for Strategic and International Studies, 2013.

41. Yereth Rosen, "Murkowski, King seek to enlist other senators in an Arctic caucus," *Alaska Dispatch News*, March 4, 2015, available from *www.adn.com/arctic/article/murkowski-king- seek-enlist-other-senators-arctic-caucus/2015/03/04/.*

42. *National Defense Authorization Act for Fiscal Year 2016: Conference Report to Accompany H.R. 1735*, 114th Congress, 1st

Session, U.S. House of Representatives, Report 114-270, September 29, 2015, Washington, DC: U.S. Government Publishing Office, p. 701.

43. John P. Holdren, "Ambassador Mark Brzezinski Appointed Executive Director of the Arctic Executive Steering Committee," The White House Blog, August 13, 2015, available from *https://www.whitehouse.gov/blog/2015/08/13/ambassador-mark-brzezinski-appointed-executive-officer-arctic-executive-steering.*

44. Arctic Executive Steering Committee, *2015 Year in Review: Progress Report on the Implementation of the National Strategy for the Arctic Region*, Washington, DC: Executive Office of the President of the United States, March 2016, p. 4.

45. The White House Official website, "President Obama's Trip to Alaska," available from *https://www.whitehouse.gov/2015-alaska-trip.* Kotzebue is 1,060 miles northwest of Juneau, Alaska.

46. O'Rourke, *Coast Guard Polar Icebreaker Modernization*, pp. 7-8.

47. Office of the Press Secretary, "FACT SHEET: President Obama Announces New Investments to Enhance Safety and Security in the Changing Arctic," Washington, DC: The White House, available from *https://www.whitehouse.gov/the-press-office/2015/09/01/fact-sheet-president-obama-announces-new-investments-enhance-safety-and.*

48. Christopher Gray, *Fleet Arctic Operations Game: Game Report*, Newport, RI: U.S. Naval War College, November 14, 2011, p. 27.

49. "Murkowski Stresses Need for Deep Water Port in the Arctic," Press Release, United States Senator for Alaska Lisa Murkowski, March 2, 2016, available from *www.murkowski.senate.gov/public/index.cfm/pressreleases?ContentRecord_id=38BBA102-8304-49A7-90AF-792EDEDC5605.*

50. U.S. Congress, House of Representatives, Committee on Foreign Affairs, Joint Hearing, *Charting the Arctic: Security, Economic, and Resource Opportunities: Hearings before the Subcommittee*

on Europe, Eurasia, and Emerging Threats and the Subcommittee on the Western Hemisphere, 114th Cong., 1st sess., November 17, 2015, pp. 4-7, available from *https://foreignaffairs.house.gov/hearing/joint-subcommittee-hearing-charting-the-arctic-security-economic-and-re-source-opportunities/*.

51. *Ibid.*, p. 2.

52. *Ibid.*, p. 41.

53. *Ibid.*, pp. 45-46.

54. *Ibid.*, p. 46.

55. "Thule Air Base," Military Bases.US, available from *www.militarybases.us/air-force/thule-air-base/*.

56. North American Aerospace Defense Command, Office of History, *A Brief History of NORAD*, Peterson Air Force Base, CO: Headquarters, North American Aerospace Defense Command, December 31, 2013, pp. 4-7.

57. For a detailed examination of U.S. military forces in the Arctic, see Office of the Under-Secretary of Defense (Policy), U.S. Department of Defense (DoD), *Report to Congress on Arctic Operations and the Northwest Passage*, Washington, DC: U.S. Department of Defense, May 2011, pp. 22-25; and U.S. Government Accountability Office, *Arctic Planning: DOD Expects to Play a Supporting Role to Other Federal Agencies and Has Efforts Under Way to Address Capability Needs and Update Plans: Report to Congressional Committees*, GAO-15-566, Washington, DC: U.S. Government Accountability Office, pp. 15-27, June 2015.

58. Julian E. Barnes, "Arctic Passage Opens Challenges for U.S. Military," *The Wall Street Journal*, January 12, 2014, available from *www.wsj.com/articles/SB10001424052702303330204579250522717106330*.

59. Alaskan Command (ALCOM), "History," Joint Base Elmendorf-Richardson, April 2, 2015, available from *www.jber.af.mil/Units/AlaskanCommand.aspx*.

60. Steven Beardsley, "Navy Aircraft Returning to former Cold War base in Iceland," *Stars and Stripes*, February 9, 2016, available from *www.stripes.com/news/navy-aircraft-returning-to-former-cold-war-base-in-iceland-1.393156*.

61. Michelle Tan, "Army halts cuts to airborne brigade," *Army Times*, March 22, 2016, available from *www.armytimes. com/story/military/pentagon/2016/03/22/army-halts-cuts-airborne-brigade/82100776/*.

62. Tara Copp, "Arctic heats up over Army cuts to cold weather airborne brigade," *Stars and Stripes*, October 30, 2015, available from *https://www.stripes.com/news/arctic-heats-up-over-army-cuts-to-cold-weather-airborne-brigade-1.376229*.

63. Michelle Tan, "'CTC on wheels' boosts largest U.S. Army Alaska exercise in 15 years," *Army Times*, August 7, 2016, *https://www.armytimes.com/story/military/2016/08/07/ctc-wheels-boosts-largest-us-army-alaska-exercise-15-years/88311238/*.

64. Meghann Myers, "Arctic naval exercise not a hedge against Russia, officials say," *Navy Times*, March 2, 2016, available from *www.navytimes.com/story/military/2016/03/02/arctic-naval-exercise-not-hedge-against-russia-officials-say/81217804/*.

65. Julian E. Barnes, "Cold War Echoes Under the Arctic Ice: American Naval Exercise Using a Russian Submarine Takes on New Importance," *The Wall Street Journal*, March 25, 2014, available from *www.wsj.com/articles/SB10001424052702304679404579461630946609454*.

66. Gerard O'Dwyer, "NATO Rejects Direct Arctic Presence," Atlantic Council, NATOSource blog, May 30, 2013, reprinted from *Defense News*, May 29, 2013, available from *www.atlanticcouncil.org/blogs/natosource/nato-rejects-direct-arctic-presence*.

67. U.S. Government Accountability Office, *Arctic Planning*, pp. 13-15.

68. U.S. Department of Defense (DoD), *Arctic Strategy*, p. 13; also see U.S. Government Accountability Office, *Arctic Planning*, p. 17.

69. U.S. Government Accountability Office, *Arctic Planning*, pp. 16-17.

70. Andreas Østhagen, "Arctic Security: Hype, Nuances and Dilemmas," The Arctic Institute, May 27, 2015, available from *www.thearcticinstitute.org/arctic-security-hype-nuances-dilemmas-russia/*.

71. *Ibid.*

72. O'Rourke, *Changes in the Arctic*, p. 55.

73. Su Ping and Marc Lanteigne, "China's Developing Arctic Policies: Myths and Misconceptions," *Journal of China and International Relations*, Vol. 3, No. 1, 2015, p. 12; Anne-Marie Brady, "Polar Stakes: China's Polar Activities as a Benchmark for Intentions," *China Brief*, Vol. 12, Iss. 14, available from *www.jamestown. org/programs/chinabrief/single/?tx_ttnews[tt_news]=39647#.V1I-77uRL6jU*.

74. Anne-Marie Brady, "China's Undeclared Arctic Foreign Policy," *Polar Initiative Policy Brief Series Arctic 2014: Who Gets a Voice and Why it Matters*, Washington, DC: Wilson Center Polar Initiative, September 2014, p. 2.

75. *Ibid.*, p. 3.

76. Quote is from the unofficial translation of the official Chinese text, "National Security Law of the People's Republic of China (Passed on July 1, 2015 at the 15th meeting of the Standing Committee of the 12th National People's Congress)," China Law Translate, July, 1, 2015, available from *chinalawtranslate. com/2015nsl/?lang=en*, the original Chinese text is available from *www.chinadaily.com.cn/hqcj/zgjj/2015-07-01/content_13912103.html*.

77. Interview conducted by the author with a confidential source, Shanghai, June 2016; Gang Chen, "China's Emerging Arctic Strategy," *The Polar Journal*, Vol. 2, No. 2, December 2012, p. 367.

78. "Video Message by Foreign Minister Wang Yi At the Opening Ceremony of the Third Arctic Circle Assembly," Minis-

try of Foreign Affairs of the People's Republic of China, October 17, 2015, available from *www.fmprc.gov.cn/mfa_eng/zxxx_662805/ t1306857.shtml.*

79. "Arctic Circle: 2015 Assembly Program: Reykjavík, October 15-18, 2015," Arctic Circle, n.d., p. 4, available from *www. arcticcircle.org/Media/2015arcticcircleprogram01.pdf.*

80. Keynote Speech by Vice Foreign Minister Zhang Ming at the China Country Session of the Third Arctic Circle Assembly, Ministry of Foreign Affairs of the People's Republic of China, October 17, 2015, available from *cc.bingj.com/cache. aspx?q=www.fmprc.gov.cn%2fmfa_eng%2fwjbxw%2ft1306858. shtml&d=4717881498669130&mkt=en-US&setlang=en-US&w=VsKb8bxXmwhhceLGIGRNvz_Ci7W64ngB.*

81. *Ibid.*

82. *Ibid.*

83. *Ibid.*

84. Brady, "China's Undeclared Arctic Foreign Policy," p. 3; Elizabeth C. Economy, "Beijing's Arctic Play: Just the Tip of the Iceberg," Council on Foreign Relations blog, Asia Unbound, April 4, 2014, available from *blogs.cfr.org/asia/2014/04/04/beijings-arctic-play-just-the-tip-of-the-iceberg/*; Linda Jakobson and Jingchao Peng, "China's Arctic Aspirations," *SIPRI Policy Paper*, No. 34, November 2013, Stockholm International Peace Research Institute, p. 23; Caitlin Campbell, "China and the Arctic: Objectives and Obstacles," *Staff Research Report*, Washington DC: US-China Economic and Security Review Commission, April 13, 2012, p. 3; Marc Lanteigne, "China's Emerging Arctic Strategies: Economics and Institutions," *Occasional Papers*, Institute of International Affairs, Centre for Arctic Policy Studies, University of Iceland, 2015, p. 35.

85. Lanteigne, p. 11; Campbell, pp. 3-4.

86. Brady, "China's Undeclared Arctic Foreign Policy," p. 3.

87. Malte Humpert, *The Future of Arctic Shipping: A New Silk Road for China?* Washington, DC: The Arctic Institute, Center for Circumpolar Studies, November 13, 2013, pp. 6, 10.

88. Linyan Huang, Frédéric Lasserre, and Olga Alexeeva, "Is China's interest for the Arctic driven by Arctic shipping potential?" *Asian Geographer*, Vol. 32, Iss. 1, 2015, p. 67.

89. For analysis of Chinese discussions of the Arctic prior to China's observer status in the Arctic Council, see David Curtis Wright, "The Dragon Eyes the Top of the World: Arctic Policy Debate and Discussion in China," *The China Maritime Study No. 8*, Newport, RI: China Maritime Studies Institute, U.S. Naval War College, August 2011.

90. Kai Sun, "Beyond the Dragon and the Panda: Understanding China's Engagement in the Arctic," *Asia Policy*, Vol. 18, July 2014, p. 2.

91. Cheng Zhang and Deming Huang, "Zhongguo beiji quanyi weihu lujing yu celue xuanze" ("The Maintenance Route and Strategy Choice of China's Rights and Interests"), *Zhengzhi yu falu (Politics and Law)*, No. 6, 2015, pp. 74, 76.

92. Zhirong Yang, "Beiji hangdao quannian kaitonghou shijie dijia zhanlue geju de bianhua yanjiu," ("Changes in World Geostrategic situation and countermeasures after the All-year-open of Arctic Channel"), *Guofang keji (National Defense Science & Technology)*, Vol. 36, No. 2, April 2015, p. 11; also Zhang and Huang, p. 76.

93. Zhenfu Li, Xue You, and Wenya Wang, "Zhongguo beiji hangxian duoceng zhanlue tixi yanjiu" ("Study of Multilayer-Strategy System for China's Approach to the Arctic Route"), *Zhanlue yu zhengce (Strategy and Policy)*, No. 4, 2015, p. 32; Sasa Li, "Xin Eluosi de beiji zhanlue" ("Arctic Strategy of Russia"), *Jilin gongcheng jichu shifandazue yuanxue bao (Journal of Jilin Teachers Institute of Engineering and Technology)*, No. 9, 2014, p. 79.

94. Zhenfu Li, Wenya Wang, and Jing Zhu, "Beiji hanxian zai wo guo 'yidai yilu' jianshe zhong de zuoyong yanjiu" ("The Study of the Role of the Arctic Route in 'One Belt One Road' Construction"), *Yatai Jingji (Asia-Pacific Economy)*, No. 3, 2015, p. 36.

95. Sun Tzu, *The Art of War*, New York: Chartwell Books, 2012, p. 21.

96. Chenguang Wang and Kai Sun, "Yuwai guojia canyu beiji shiwu yu jiqi dui Zhongguo de qishi" ("Non-Arctic States' Participation in Arctic Affairs and Its Implications for China"), *Guoji Luntan (International Forum)*, Vol. 17, No. 1, January 2015, p. 33.

97. Kai Sun and Chenguang Wang, "Guojia liyi shijiaoxia de ZhongE beiji hezuo" ("Analysis of Sino-Russia Arctic Cooperation in the Perspective of National Interests"), *Dongbeiya Luntan (Northeast Asia Forum)*, No. 6, 2014, p. 34.

98. Zhang and Huang, p. 77.

99. Jianping Ruan, "'Jin beiji guojia' haishi 'beiji liyouguanzhe'? Zhongguo canyu beiji de shenfen sikao" ("'Near-Arctic State' or 'Arctic Stakeholder'? Thinking about China's Identity in Participation in Arctic Affairs"), *Guoji Luntan (International Forum)*, Vol. 18, No. 1, January 2016, p. 51.

100. Zhirong Yang, p. 8; Jingyu Li and Chenya Zhang, "ZhongE liangguo hezuo kaifai kaituo shijie dongbei fangxiang haishang sichou zhi lu de gouxiang" ("The Strategic Conception of Sino-Russia Joint Development of the 21st Century Maritime Silk Road to the Direction of Northeast"), *Dongbeiya Luntan (Northeast Asia Forum)*, No. 3, 2015, p. 76.

101. Kai Sun, "Zhongguo beiji waijiao: shizhan, liyi yu jinlu" ("China's Arctic Diplomacy: Practice, Principles, and Ways Forward"), *Taipingyang xuebao (Pacific Journal)*, Vol. 23, No. 5, May 2015, p. 37.

102. *Ibid.*, pp. 42-44.

103. Ningning Zhao and Leizhao Wu, "Meguo yu beiji bingyang gonghai yuyue zhili: liyi kaoliang ji zhengce shijian?" ("America and Fishery Governance in the Central Arctic Ocean: Interest Considerations and Policy Practice"), *Shihuizhuyi yanjiu (Socialism Studies)*, No. 1, 2016, p. 132; Li, You, and Wang, p. 30.

104. Chenguang Wang, "Beiji zhili fazhihua yu Zongguo de shenfen zuoli" ("Arctic Governance under the Rule of Law and China's National Identity"), *Guoji zhil pinglun (Global Governance)*, No. 1, 2016, pp. 81-84.

105. Li Yibo, "Meiguo beiji zhanlue de xindongxiang jiqi yinxiang" ("On the New Trends of U.S. Arctic Strategy and Its Implications"), *Taipingyang xuebao (Pacific Journal)*, Vol. 22, No. 6, June 2014, p. 79.

106. Li, You, and Wang, pp. 31-35; Fangfang Wan, "Eluosi beiji kaifa zhengce yingxiang yinsu xiang" ("The Influence Factors Analysis of Russia's Arctic Development Policy"), *Eluosi Xuekan (Russian Studies)*, Vol. 6, 2013, p. 16.

107. Jian Yang, "The Arctic Governance and the Interactions between Arctic and Non-Arctic Countries," in Leiv Lunde, Jian Yang, and Iselin Stensdal, eds., *Asian Countries and the Arctic Future*, Singapore: World Scientific, 2015, pp. 45-46.

108. Li and Zhang, p. 83.

109. Ruan, p. 48.

110. Wright, "The Dragon Eyes the Top of the World, pp. 4-5; Bo Xin, "Cong zhanlue cong hao dao liyi bianjie—pandian EMei Beiji boai de: 'jiuhen xin chou?'" ("From strategy to border interests—U.S.-Russia interactions: 'old hate or new hate?'"), *Junqing Guanzhu (Military Concerns)*, 2016, p. 20.

111. Zhirong Yang, p. 8.

112. *Ibid.*, pp. 10-11.

113. Yibo, pp. 79-80.

114. Deng Beixi and Zhang Xia, "EMei beiji guanxi shijiaoxia de beiji dijiazhengzhi fazhang fenxi" ("Analysis on Arctic Geopolitical Development from Perspective of U.S.-Russian Arctic Relations"), *Taipingyang xuebao (Pacific Journal)*, Vol. 23, No. 11, November 2015, p. 43.

115. Jiang Ye, "On China's Role in Arctic Governance—with the Case Study of China's Reaction during US Arctic Council Chairmanship from 2015 to 2017," *Academics*, No. 1, January 2016, pp. 259, 261.

116. P. Whitney Lackenbauer and James Manicom, "Asian States and the Arctic: National Perspectives on Regional Governance," in Leif Christian Jensen and Geir Hønneland, eds., *Handbook of the Politics of the Arctic*, Cheltenham, UK: Edward Elgar Publishing, Limited, 2015, p. 518.

117. Frédéric Lasserre, "China and the Arctic: Threat or Cooperation Potential for Canada?" *China Papers No. 11*, Canadian International Council, June 2010, p. 9; on Canada's role in the Arctic Council more generally also see Fenge, "The Arctic Council," pp. 7-35.

118. Wright, "The Dragon Eyes the Top of the World, pp. 32-38; David Curtis Wright, "China's Growing Interest in the Arctic," *Journal of Military and Strategic Studies*, Vol. 15, No. 2, 2013, pp. 50-59; Rob Huebert, "Canada and China in the Arctic: A Work in Progress," *Meridian Newsletter*, Canadian Polar Commission, Fall/Winter 2011-Spring/Summer 2012, available from *www.polarcom.gc.ca/eng/content/meridian-newsletter-fallwinter-2011-spring-summer-2012-0*.

119. P. Whitney Lackenbauer and James Manicom, "Canada's Northern Strategy and East Asian Interests in the Arctic," East Asia-Arctic Relations: Boundary, Security and International Politics, Paper No. 5, The Centre for International Governance Innovation, December 2013, p. 8, available from *https://www.cigionline.org/sites/default/files/no5_4.pdf*.

120. Eric Haun, "China Issues Guidance on Arctic Navigation," Marine Link, May 10, 2016, available from *www.marinelink.com/news/navigation-guidance409448.aspx*.

121. Nathan Vanderklippe, "China reveals plan to ship cargo across Canada's Northwest Passage," *The Globe and Mail*, April 20, 2016, available from *www.theglobeandmail.com/news/world/china-reveals-plans-to-ship-cargo-across-canadas-northwest-passage/article29691054/*.

122. Letter from the U.S. Ambassador to Canada David Wilkins to the Canadian Deputy Assistant Minister for North America Peter Boehm, October 27, 2006, available from *www.state. gov/documents/organization/98836.pdf.*

123. "Foreign Ministry Spokesperson Hua Chunying's Regular Press Conference on April 20, 2016," Ministry of Foreign Affairs of the People's Republic of China, April 20, 2016, available from *www.fmprc.gov.cn/mfa_eng/xwfw_665399/s2510_665401/ t1357177.shtml.*

124. Evan Dyer, "Obama and Trudeau pledge to protect a warming Arctic," CBC News, March 11, 2016, available from *www.cbc.ca/news/politics/us-canada-arctic-protection-1.3486062.*

125. "Foreign Ministry Spokesperson Hong Lei's Regular Press Conference on November 20, 2015," Embassy of the People's Republic of China in the Republic of Iceland, November 20, 2015, available from *is.china-embassy.org/eng/fyrth/t1316837.htm.*

126. Vladimir Soldatkin and Olesya Astakhova, "UPDATE 2-Russia's Yamal LNG gets round sanctions with $12 bln Chinese loan deal," Reuters, April 29, 2016, available from *uk.reuters.com/ article/russia-china-yamal-idUKL5N17V2G8.*

127. Vladimir Putin, "Meeting of the Security Council on state policy in the Arctic," Official Internet Resources of the President of Russia, April 22, 2014, available from *eng.kremlin.ru/news/7065.*

128. Ekaterina Klimenko, "Russia's Evolving Arctic Strategy: Drivers, Challenges and New Opportunities," *SIPRI Policy Paper,* No. 42, September 2014, pp. 1, 3.

129. Campbell, p. 5; Lasserre, p. 7.

130. "Junkeyuan fashi zhanlue pinglun baogao: Zhongguo mianlin san da taikong weixie" ("Army Research Institute Released a Strategic Assessment Report: China Faces Three Major Space Threats"), Sina Military, June 19, 2014, available from *mil. news.sina.com.cn/2014-06-19/1657785793.html.*

131. Katarzyna Zysk, "Asian Interests in the Arctic: Risks and Gains for Russia," *Asia Policy*, Vol. 18, July 2014, p. 35.

132. Klimenko, p. 20.

133. Alexander Gabuev, "A 'Soft Alliance'? Russia-China Relations After the Ukraine Crisis," *Policy Brief*, London, UK: European Council on Foreign Relations, February 2015, available from *www.ecfr.eu/page/-/ECFR126_-_A_Soft_Alliance_Russia-China_Relations_After_the_Ukraine_Crisis.pdf*.

134. Deng Beixi, "Arctic Geopolitics: The Impact of U.S.-Russian Relations on Chinese-Russian Cooperation in the Arctic," *Russia in Global Affairs*, No. 138, March 30, 2016, available from *eng.globalaffairs.ru/number/Arctic-Geopolitics-18074*.

135. Katya Golubkova and Denis Pinchuk, "Kremlin pivot to China slowed as projects delayed," Reuters, August 27, 2015, available from *uk.reuters.com/article/2015/08/27/uk-russia-china-projects-idUKKCN0QW15T20150827*.

136. "Russia Turning to China for Long-Term Funding," Oil & Gas 360, September 29, 2015, available from *www.oilandgas360.com/russia-turning-to-china-for-long-term-funding/*.

137. James Marson, "Russian Natural-Gas Project Gets Funding from China," *The Wall Street Journal*, April 29, 2016, available from *www.wsj.com/articles/russian-natural-gas-project-gets-funding-from-china-1461934776*.

138. Klimenko, p. 23.

139. Trude Pettersen, "First Chinese Merchant Ship on Northern Sea Route," Barents Observer, August 12, 2013, available from *barentsobserver.com/en/arctic/2013/08/first-chinese-merchant-ship-northern-sea-route-12-08*.

140. Tom Roseth, "Russia's China Policy in the Arctic," *Strategic Analysis*, Vol. 38, No. 6, 2015, p. 853.

141. *Ibid*.

142. Trude Pettersen, "Russia and China sign agreement on Belkomur railroad," Barents Observer, September 4, 2015, available from *barentsobserver.com/en/business/2015/09/russia-and-china-sign-agreement-belkomur-railroad-04-09.*

143. Vitaly Chernov, "Phantoms of Russian Infrastructure—2015," Port News, December 22, 2015, available from *en.portnews.ru/comments/2065/.*

144. Ping and Lanteigne, p. 10.

145. Cited in Kai Sun, "China and the Arctic: China's Interests and Participation in the Region," in Kimie Hara and Ken Coates, eds., *East Asia-Arctic Relations: Boundary, Security and International Politics,* Toronto: Centre for International Governance Innovation, 2014, p. 40; also see Huang, Lasserre, and Alexeeva, p. 61.

146. Li, Wang, and Zhu, p. 36.

147. Huang, Lasserre, and Alexeeva, p. 66.

148. Jia Liu, ed., "China Begins 7th Arctic Expedition," Chinese Academy of Sciences, July 12, 2016, available from *english. cas.cn/newsroom/china_research/201607/t20160712_165563.shtml.*

149. "China to further explore Antarctic, deep sea this year," Xinhua, February 9, 2016, available from *news.xinhuanet.com/ english/2016-02/09/c_135086260.htm.*

150. For example, Woods Hole Research Center in the United States has been cooperating with several Russian scientific institutions; see the previous Polaris Project teams available from *www. thepolarisproject.org/team/.*

151. Sun and Wang, "Guojia liyi shijiaoxia de ZhongE beiji hezuo," pp. 31-32.

152. *Ibid.,* pp. 32.

153. Li and Zhang, p. 82.

154. Long Zhao, "Beifang hangdao zhengce shanbian yu Eluosi 'yuanzexing tuoxie?' zhiliguan" ("The Policy Change in the North Channel and Russia Selective Governance View"), *Siboliya Yanjiu (Siberian Studies)*, Vol. 42, No. 1, 2015, p. 30; Vesa Virtanen, "The Arctic in world politics. The United States, Russia, and China in the Arctic—implications for Finland," Weatherhead Center for International Affairs, Harvard University, July 17, 2013, p. 56.

155. Cited in Roseth, p. 844.

156. Nadezhda Filimonova and Svetlana Krivokhizh, "A Russian Perspective on China's Arctic Role," *The Diplomat*, September 27, 2014, available from *thediplomat.com/2014/09/a-russian-perspective-on-chinas-arctic-role/*.

157. Roseth, p. 845.

158. Zysk, p. 34.

159. Roseth, p. 846.

160. Linda Jakobson, "China Prepares for an Ice-Free Arctic," *SIPRI Insights on Peace and Security*, No. 2010/2, March 2010, Stockholm International Peace Research Institute, p. 11.

161. "Haijun shaojiang: Kaifai beibingyang Zhongguo buke 'quefa'" ("Admiral: China should not be denied a share of Arctic Ocean development"), Zhongguo xinwen wang (China News Agency), May 3, 2010, available from *www.chinanews.com/gn/news/2010/03-05/2154039.shtml*.

162. Olya Gayazova, "China's Rights in the Marine Arctic," *The International Journal of Marine and Coastal Law*, Vol. 28, Iss. 1, 2013, pp. 61-95.

163. Zhao, p. 29; Li and Zhang, p. 28.

164. Klimenko, p. 12.

165. Douglas Quan and Vladimir Isachenkov, The Associated Press (AP), "Russia submits claim for 1.2-million square kilometres of the Arctic . . . including the North Pole," *National Post*, August 4, 2015, available from *news.nationalpost.com/news/world/*

russia-submits-claim-for-vast-arctic-seabed-territories-at-united-nations.

166. Andrew E. Kramer, "Russia Presents Revised Claim of Arctic Territory to the United Nations," *The New York Times*, February 9, 2016, available from *www.nytimes.com/2016/02/10/world/europe/russia-to-present-revised-claim-of-arctic-territory-to-the-united-nations.html.*

167. Elizabeth Wishnick, "In Search of the 'Other' in Asia: Russia-China relations revisited," *The Pacific Review*, forthcoming 2017, published online July 7, 2016, available from *www.tandfonline.com/doi/full/10.1080/09512748.2016.1201129*; Gilbert Rozman, "Asia for the Asians: Why Chinese-Russian Friendship Is Here To Stay," *Foreign Affairs*, October, 29, 2014, available from *https://www.foreignaffairs.com/articles/east-asia/2014-10-29/asia-asians.*

168. Marlene Laruelle, *Russia's Arctic Strategies and the Future of the Far North*, Armonk, NY: M.E. Sharpe, 2014, p. 40.

169. Jinping Xi, "Diplomacy with Neighboring Countries Characterized by Friendship, Sincerity, Reciprocity, Inclusiveness," in the State Council Information Office, Party Literature Research Office of the CPC Central Committee, and the China International Publishing Group, producers, *Xi Jinping The Governance of China*, Beijing: Foreign Language Press, p. 326; Camilla T. N. Sørensen, "The Significance of Xi Jinping's 'Chinese Dream' for Chinese Foreign Policy: From 'Tao Guang Yang Hui' to 'Fen Fa You Wei,'" *Journal of Contemporary International Relations*, Vol. 3, No. 1, 2015, pp. 65-66.

170. Wang, "Arctic Security — An Equation with Multiple Unknowns," p. 15.

171. Brady, "China's Undeclared Arctic Foreign Policy," p. 3.

172. Filimonova and Krivokhizh.

173. Virtanen, p. 18.

174. Leiv Lunde, "The Nordic Embrace: Why the Nordic Countries Welcome Asia to the Arctic Table," *Asia Policy*, Vol. 18, July 2014, pp. 43-44.

175. Didi Kirsten Tatlow, "China and the Northern Rivalry," International Herald Tribune (IHT) Rendezvous blog, October 5, 2012, available from *rendezvous.blogs.nytimes.com/2012/10/05/ china-and-the-northern-great-game/*.

176. Ping and Lanteigne, p. 4.

177. Reuters and Kyodo News International, "Is China's Ambassador to Iceland Missing Because He Spied for Japan?" NATOSource blog, September 17, 2014, available from *www.at- lanticcouncil.org/blogs/natosource/is-china-s-ambassador-to-iceland- missing-because-he-spied-for-japan*.

178. Jesse Hastings, Edward H. Huijbens, Gustav Péturs- son, and Jennifer Smith, "Chinese Chess in the Wild West: How Icelanders View the Growing Iceland-China Relationship," The Centre for Arctic Policy Studies, Institute of International Affairs, University of Iceland, Rejkavik, 2015, p. 15.

179. Jingchao Peng and Njord Wegge, "China's bilateral diplomacy in the Arctic," *Polar Geography*, Vol. 38, No. 3, 2015, pp. 242-243.

180. "CNOOC-led consortium meets to discuss exploration offshore Iceland," Offshore, October 7, 2016, available from *www. offshore-mag.com/articles/2016/10/cnooc-led-consortium-meets-to-dis- cuss-oil-and-gas-exploration-offshore-iceland.html*.

181. Arthur Guschin, "China, Iceland and the Arctic," *The Diplomat*, May 20, 2015, available from *thediplomat.com/2015/05/ china-iceland-and-the-arctic/*.

182. Martin Breum and Jorgen Chemnitz, "No, Green- land Does Not Belong to China," *The New York Times*, February 20, 2013, available from *www.nytimes.com/2013/02/21/opinion/ no-greenland-does-not-belong-to-china.html?_r=0*.

183. Tim Boersma and Kevin Foley, "The Greenland Gold Rush: Promise and Pitfalls of Greenland's Energy and Mineral Resources," *Brookings Institution Report*, Washington, DC: The Brookings Institution, September 2014, p. 45, available from *www.*

brookings.edu/~/media/Research/Files/Reports/2014/09/24-greenland-energy-mineral-resources-boersma-foley/24-greenland-energy-mineral-resources-boersma-foley-pdf-2.pdf?la=en.

184. Jichang Lulu, "Greenland's mines could finally attract Chinese investment," China Policy Institute: Analysis, December 7, 2015, available from *blogs.nottingham.ac.uk/chinapolicyinstitute/2015/12/07/greenlands-mines-could-finally-attract-chinese-investment/.*

185. Ping and Lanteigne, pp. 4-7; Boersma and Foley, pp. 46-47.

186. Lucy Hornby, Richard Milne, and James Wilson, "Chinese group General Nice takes over Greenland mine," *Financial Times*, January 11, 2015, available from *www.ft.com/cms/s/0/22842e82-9979-11e4-a3d7-00144feabdc0.html#axzz4AiraacJW.*

187. Boersma and Foley, p. 52.

188. "Observers," Arctic Council, May 7, 2015, available from *www.arctic-council.org/index.php/en/about-us/arctic-council/observers.*

189. Arctic Council, *Arctic Council Rules of Procedure*, Tromsø, NO: Arctic Council Secretariat, 2013, p. 9, available from *https://oaarchive.arctic-council.org/bitstream/handle/11374/940/2015-09-01_Rules_of_Procedure_website_version.pdf?sequence=1&isAllowed=y.*

190. *Ibid.*

191. Matthew Willis and Duncan Depledge, "How We Learned to Stop Worrying about China's Arctic Ambitions: Understanding China's Admission to the Arctic Council, 2004-2013," in Leif Christian Jensen and Geir Hønneland, eds., *Handbook of the Politics of the Arctic*, Cheltenham, UK: Edward Elgar Publishing, Limited, 2015, p. 397.

192. Erik J. Molenaar, "Current and Prospective Roles of the Arctic Council System within the Context of the Law of the Sea," in Thomas S. Axworthy, Timo Koivurova, and Waliul Hasanat, eds., *The Arctic Council: Its Place in the Future of Arctic Governance*, Toronto: Munk-Gordon Arctic Security Program, 2012, p. 170. This was

also a concern regarding the admission of the European Union (EU), though its application for observer status was ultimately not accepted due to an ongoing bilateral dispute between the EU and and Canada over seals.

193. Kevin Xie, "Some BRICS in the Arctic: Developing Powers Look North," *Harvard International Review*, Vol. 36, No. 3, Spring 2015, p. 62.

194. Song Sang-ho, "S. Korea, Japan, China hold talks on Arctic affairs," Yonhap News Agency, April 28, 2016, available from *english.yonhapnews.co.kr/national/2016/04/28/0301000000AEN20160428003551315.html*.

195. For background, see "North Pacific Arctic Conference," East-West Center, n.d., available from *www.eastwestcenter.org/research/research-projects/north-pacific-arctic-conference*.

196. Zysk, pp. 32-33.

197. "Prime Minister Dmitry Medvedev gives an interview to Norwegian TV Company NRK," The Russian Government News, June 4, 2013, available from *government.ru/en/news/2273/*.

198. "RF budet prioritetno sotrudnichat' s Kitaem v Arktcheskoy zone—MID" ("The Russian Federation should make cooperation with China in the Arctic zone a priority"), Regnum, August 24, 2015, available from *regnum.ru/news/polit/1956304.html*.

199. Asia Pacific Foundation of Canada, "Charting Canada's Relations with Asia in the Arctic: Points of View Asia Pacific Opinion Panel," Asia Pacific Foundation of Canada, Vancouver, BC: May 14, 2013, p. 9, available from *https://www.asiapacific.ca/surveys/survey-report/charting-canadas-relations-asia-arctic*.

200. P. Whitney Lackenbauer, "Canada and the Asian Observers to the Arctic Council: Anxiety and Opportunity," *Asia Policy*, Vol. 18, July 2014, pp. 23-24.

201. Lunde, "The Nordic Embrace," p. 43.

202. Thomas Nilsen, "China-Nordic Arctic Research Center opens in Shanghai," Barents Observer, December 12, 2013, available from *barentsobserver.com/en/arctic/2013/12/china-nordic-arctic-research-center-opens-shanghai-12-12.*

203. Kim Ghattas, "Arctic Council: John Kerry steps into Arctic diplomacy," BBC News, May 14, 2013, available from *www.bbc.com/news/world-us-canada-22528594.*

204. James Kraska, "Asian States in U.S. Arctic Policy: Perceptions and Prospects," *Asian Policy*, Vol. 18, July 2014, p. 20.

205. Leiv Lunde, "Introduction: Nordic Perspectives on Asia's Arctic Interests," in Leiv Lunde, Jian Yang, and Iselin Stensdal, eds., *Asian Countries and the Arctic Future*, Singapore: World Scientific, 2015, p. 8.

206. Steven Lee Myers, "Arctic Council Adds 6 Nations as Observer States, Including China," *The New York Times*, May 15, 2013, available from *www.nytimes.com/2013/05/16/world/europe/arctic-council-adds-six-members-including-china.html.*

207. Kraska, p. 20.

208. Lunde, "Introduction," in Lunde, Yang, and Stensdal, *Asian Countries and the Arctic Future*, p. 9.

209. Arctic Council, *Arctic Council Rules of Procedure*, p. 14.

210. Willis and Depledge, p. 402.

211. Kraska, p. 21.

212. See Part II of United Nations, "United Nations Convention on the Law of the Sea," Oceans and Law of the Sea, Division for Ocean Affairs and the Law of the Sea, December 10, 1982, available from *www.un.org/depts/los/convention_agreements/texts/unclos/part2.htm.*

213. Sam LaGrone, "Chinese Warships Made 'Innocent Passage' Through U.S. Territorial Waters off Alaska," USNI News, September 3, 2015, available from *https://news.usni.org/2015/09/03/*

chinese-warships-made-innocent-passage-through-u-s-territorial-wa-
ters-off-alaska.

214. Shannon Tiezzi, "Why Did China Opt Out of the Arc-tic Climate Change Statement?" *The Diplomat,* September 1, 2015, available from *thediplomat.com/2015/09/why-did-china-opt-out-of-the-arctic-climate-change-statement/*; Office of the Spokesperson, "Joint Statement on Climate Change and the Arctic," Washing-ton, DC: U.S. Department of State, August 31, 2015, available from *arcticjournal.com/press-releases/1799/joint-statement-climate-change-and-arctic.*

215. Elizabeth Shell, "Here's what you need to know about the Arctic climate meeting," CGTN America, August 31, 2015, available from *america.cgtn.com/2015/08/31/heres-what-you-need-to-know-about-the-arctic-climate-meeting;* "Saving the Arctic? Kerry's roadmap not melting hearts in Russia, China & India," RT, Sep-tember 1, 2015, available from *https://www.rt.com/news/313975-arc-tic-conference-climate-roadmap/.*

216. Ronald A. LaBrec, "U.S. Coast Guard Unveils a New Model for Cooperation Atop the World," Defense in Depth, No-vember 2, 2015, available from *blogs.cfr.org/davidson/2015/11/02/u-s-coast-guard-unveils-a-new-model-for-cooperation-on-top-of-the-world/.*

217. "Memorandum of Understanding Between the Gov-ernment of the United States of America and the Government of the People's Republic of China on Effective Cooperation and Implementation of United Nations General Assembly Resolution 46/215 of December 20, 1991," Washington, DC: U.S. Department of State, December 3, 1993, available from *www.nmfs.noaa.gov/ia/agreements/LMR%20report/us_china_46_215_agreement.pdf.*

218. Coast Guard 17th District External Affairs Office, "Mul-timedia Release: United States and China Coast Guards Interdict Vessel for Illegally Fishing on the High Seas," U.S. Coast Guard Newsroom, June 3, 2014, available from *cc.bingj.com/cache.aspx?q=Multimedia+Release%3a+United+States+and+China+Coast+Guards+Interdict+Vessel+for+Illegally+Fishing+on+the+High+Seas&d=4769322295957351&mkt=en-US&setlang=en-US&w=mSeVccHTRpt41jff2njBhIC0eZ7gUG6h.*

219. Min Pan and Henry P. Huntington, "A Precautionary Approach to Fisheries in the Central Arctic Ocean: Policy, Science, and China," *Marine Policy*, Vol. 63, January 2016, p. 154; Office of the Spokesperson, "Arctic Nations Sign Declaration to Prevent Unregulated Fishing in the Central Arctic Ocean," Washington, DC: U.S. Department of State, July 16, 2015, available from *arcticjournal.com/press-releases/2427/arctic-nations-sign-declaration-prevent-unregulated-fishing-central-arctic-ocean*.

220. Robert J. Papp, Jr., "Statement of Admiral Robert J. Papp, Jr., Special Representative for the Arctic, U.S. Department of State, Before the Committee on Foreign Affairs, Subcommittees on Europe, Eurasia, and Emerging Threats, and Western Hemisphere, U.S. House of Representatives, November 17, 2015," Washington, DC: U.S. Department of State, p. 9, available from *docs.house.gov/meetings/FA/FA14/20151117/104201/HHRG-114-FA14-Wstate-PappR-20151117.pdf*.

221. Mary Sweeters, "Meeting to Determine Future of Arctic Fishing Delivers Mixed Results," Greenpeace, December 7, 2015, available from *www.greenpeace.org/usa/meeting-to-determine-future-of-arctic-fishing-delivers-mixed-results/*.

222. Peng and Wegge, pp. 240-241.

223. *Ibid.*, p. 241; also see Virtanen, pp. 55-56.

224. Jonathan G. Odom, "A China in the Bull Shop? Comparing the Rhetoric Of A Rising China With The Reality Of The International Law Of The Sea," *Ocean and Coastal Law Journal,* Vol. 17, No. 2, 2011, p. 223; Dean Cheng, "Winning without Fighting: Chinese Legal Warfare," *Backgrounder, No. 2692*, The Heritage Foundation, May 18, 2012, available from *www.heritage.org/research/reports/2012/05/winning-without-fighting-chinese-legal-warfare*.

225. Shiloh Rainwater, "Race To The North: China's Arctic Strategy and Its Implications," *Naval War College Review*, Vol. 66, No. 2, Spring 2013, p. 74.

226. Sandra Cassotta, Kamrul Hossain, Jingzheng Ren, and Michael Evan Goodsite, "Climate Change and China as a Global

Emerging Regulatory Sea Power in the Arctic Ocean: Is China a Threat for Arctic Ocean Security?" *Beijing Law Review*, Vol. 6, No. 3, September 2015, p. 206; Andrea Beck, "China's strategy in the Arctic: a case of lawfare?" *The Polar Journal*, Vol. 4, Iss. 2, 2014, p. 313; Gayazova, p. 95.

227. Jakobson and Peng, p. 22.

228. Cassotta *et al.*, pp. 202-204; Beck, p. 311; Chen, p. 369. These authors all rely on Aaron Friedberg's definition of China's grand strategy, as discussed in Aaron L. Friedberg, *A Contest for Supremacy: China, America, and the Struggle for Mastery in Asia*, New York: W.W. Norton & Company, 2012.

229. Chen, pp. 365-368.

230. International Crisis Group, "Stirring Up the South China Sea (I)," *Asia Report No. 223,* April 23, 2012, p. 4, available from *https://www.crisisgroup.org/asia/south-east-asia/south-china-sea/stirring-south-china-sea-i*.

231. Stephen Blank and Younkyoo Kim, "The Arctic and New Security Challenges in Asia," *Pacific Focus*, Vol. 28, Iss. 3, December 2013, p. 322; Stephen Blank, "The Arctic: China's Third Silk Road," China Policy Institute: Analysis, March 11, 2015, available from *https://cpianalysis.org/2015/03/11/the-arctic-chinas-third-silk-road/*.

232. Jonathan Odom, "How China Shot Down Its Own A2/AD Lawfare Strategy," *The National Interest,* October 8, 2015, available from *nationalinterest.org/feature/how-china-shot-down-its-own-a2-ad-lawfare-strategy-14037?page=3*.

233. "Foreign Ministry Spokesperson Lu Kang's Regular Press Conference on May 11, 2016," Ministry of Foreign Affairs of the People's Republic of China, May 11, 2016, available from *www.fmprc.gov.cn/mfa_eng/xwfw_665399/s2510_665401/t1362394.shtml*.

234. Willis and Depledge, p. 397.

235. Elizabeth Wishnick, "The New China-Russia-U.S. Triangle," *NBR Analysis Brief,* The National Bureau of Asian Research, December 16, 2015, pp. 1-2.

236. Rensselaer Lee and Artyom Lukin, *Russia's Far East: New Dynamics in Asia-Pacific and Beyond*, Boulder, CO: Lynne Rienne Publishers, Incorporated, 2015, p. 127.

237. Kurt M. Campbell, Jay Gulledge, J.R. McNeill, John Podesta, Peter Ogden, Leon Fuerth, R. James Woolsey, Alexander T.J. Lennon, Julianne Smith, Richard Weitz, and Derek Mix, *The Age of Consequences: The Foreign Policy and National Security Implications of Global Climate Change*, Washington, DC: Center for Strategic and International Studies and Center for a New America, 2007, p. 7.

238. German Advisory Council on Global Change, *World in Transition: Climate Change as a Security Risk*, London, UK: Earthscan, 2007, p. 149; Joanna Lewis, "Climate Change Challenges and China's Foreign Policy," in Guoguang Wu, ed., *China's Challenges to Human Security: Foreign Relations and Global Implications*, London, UK: Routledge, 2012, p. 60.

239. Chris Buckley, "Chinese Report on Climate Change Depicts Somber Scenarios," *The New York Times*, November 29, 2015, available from *www.nytimes.com/2015/11/30/world/asia/chinese-report-on-climate-change-depicts-somber-scenarios.html*.

240. Oran R. Young, "Arctic Tipping Points: Governance in Turbulent Times," *Ambio*, Vol. 41, Iss. 1, February 2012, p. 80.

241. Kristian Åtland, "Interstate Relations in the Arctic: An Emerging Security Dilemma?" *Comparative Strategy*, Vol. 33, No. 2, 2014, pp. 162-163.

242. Heather A. Conley and Matthew Melino, *An Arctic Redesign: Recommendations to Rejuvenate the Arctic Council*, Washington, DC: Center for Strategic and International Studies, February 2016, p. 17.

243. Paul Arthur Berkman, Lloyd N. Axworthy, and Oran R. Young, "Escalating Tensions Challenge U.S. Chairmanship of the Arctic Council," *The World Post*, June 5, 2015, available from *www.huffingtonpost.com/prof-paul-arthur-berkman/escalating-tensions-chall_b_7002970.html*.

U.S. ARMY WAR COLLEGE

Major General William E. Rapp
Commandant

*****

STRATEGIC STUDIES INSTITUTE
and
U.S. ARMY WAR COLLEGE PRESS

Director
Professor Douglas C. Lovelace, Jr.

Director of Research
Dr. Steven K. Metz

Author
Dr. Elizabeth Wishnick

Editor for Production
Dr. James G. Pierce

Publications Assistant
Ms. Denise J. Kersting

*****

Composition
Mrs. Jennifer E. Nevil

www.ingramcontent.com/pod-product-compliance
Lightning Source LLC
Chambersburg PA
CBHW062011280526
45787CB00005B/2064